Praise

'At last, a book that will be genuinely helpful to founders! Rachel's been a founder, then coached founders for over two decades, and her understanding of the challenges we face is second to none. Leading a fast-growing start-up is an exhilarating and bumpy ride and *The Founder's Survival Guide* makes it just a little smoother. Buy it and keep it by your desk!'

— **Melanie Travis,** founder, Andie Swim

'Required reading for any founder looking to successfully traverse the challenges of start-up and scale-up. Rachel understands founders and what makes them tick, and her book is packed full of insights, tips and tactics that will enable them to not just survive but to thrive.'

— **Rob Kaplan,** founder, Circulate Capital

'This is an essential resource for any founder, a handbook to turn to when things get tough. All founders make mistakes. This book tells you how to dig yourself out of every hole you will fall into on your business journey. Heed Rachel's advice and you might even avoid falling into so many.'

— **Polly MacKenzie,** former CEO, Demos

'Rachel shares her wisdom generously, expecting nothing back but the joy she gets from helping others be successful. I am privileged to have her as my coach and was one of the first to read this book. When I started to suffer from being a Brave Warrior while scaling my company, her wisdom helped me to see my strengths and weaknesses and manage them. My killer shots were my greatest assets but they started to become my greatest liabilities and I didn't know how to use them. *The Founder's Survival Guide* will help you survive and thrive! You're lucky to have this book by your side.'

— **Dilek Dayinlarli,** founder, ScaleX Ventures

'This book is actually more like a user manual... to *myself*. Rachel is truly a master when it comes to making big concepts easy to grasp. This book hands you both a framework and a Toolbox to unlock the best leader you can be for every situation. If you're exiting the messy, beginning stage as a company and you're ready to grow up as a CEO, please make this book your business bible.'

— **Rachael King,** founder, Pod People

'The ideas in this book have been central to my success as the founder of a scaling business. Buy it. Keep it by your bed. Turn to it whenever things get hairy.'

— **Petronella West,** founder, Investment Quorum

THE
FOUNDER'S
SURVIVAL
GUIDE

Lead your business from
start-up to **scale-up** to **grown-up**

RACHEL E TURNER

R^ethink

First published in Great Britain in 2022
by Rethink Press (www.rethinkpress.com)

© Copyright Rachel Turner

Illustrations by Tom Russell, Inky Thinking, www.inkythinking.com

For the four people who have made me who I am: Roger, Jan, Francesco and William, you are my world.

Contents

The Founder's Survival Toolbox

Introduction

This book is a love letter to founders. I come from a family of founders; I've been one myself, and I've spent more than twenty years coaching and advising them. I have huge affection for the unique combination of skill, mindset and motivation that makes somebody want to start their own business.

Founding and scaling a business is isolating and stressful. You need to be a visionary leader, skilled manager, operations genius, salesperson par excellence and technical whizz-kid, often all on the same day. You need to get twenty-seven hours of work done in every twenty-four-hour day, have the answers to everyone's problems and stay both honest and fearless. Oh, and you'll probably need to do it for between six and ten years.

Very few founders survive the scale-up journey, let alone thrive during it. Through my business, VC Talent Lab, I spend my life coaching founders of venture capital-backed businesses to be the ones who make it. My job is to enable founders to survive and thrive so that they can lead profitable, healthy and successful businesses and enjoy the journey along the way. The purpose of this book is to show you how to do the same.

My story

I launched my first venture, a music PR business, during my gap year when I was eighteen. My then ex-boyfriend (now in fact my husband of over twenty years, but that's another story) was running club nights in Italy and I convinced him to let me do some PR for him. I hadn't a clue what I was doing, but I was keen, willing to work for expenses and had the gift of the gab, so it worked OK. He introduced me to a company that was then the largest distributor of dance music in Italy. I convinced them to let me do PR for them too, and they gave me a couple of boxes of records and sent me on my way. Within three months, they had seen a huge surge in their UK sales and decided it was because of the work I'd done. It's likely their sales were more to do with a change in music trends than anything I had done, but I wasn't going to tell them that when they asked me to be a director of, and equity partner in, their new UK subsidiary a couple of months after my nineteenth birthday.

So there I was, a director of my first limited company while still in my teens. I was flying high. I cancelled my place at university, got business cards printed and settled in to be successful at my new office in West London. After two years I walked out, blaming my business partners for my disenchantment with the role.

Within six weeks, I'd started my next business, a music management company, with my then partner, a high-profile DJ. The company went on to manage bookings for twenty of the most in-demand DJs in Europe, ran a hugely successful club night in London and a global touring operation. We launched a record label backed by a six-figure investment from a large German distributor, and brought in a seven-figure annual income. We had a big house in the countryside, drove flash cars and turned left when we got onto planes.

By the age of twenty-six, I was mentally, physically and emotionally broken. I worked crazy hours and had gained sixty pounds. I was frustrated with everyone I worked with, overwhelmed with all the responsibility and angry with myself. My stress levels were through the roof, my mood swings uncontrollable and my vicious tongue legendary. I knew this time that I was the problem, but I couldn't work out what to do about it. I walked out of that business too, signed everything over to my ex-partner and left the music industry for good.

I spent the next four years trying to understand why I blew up that business and my life with it. I decided to study psychology at university, went on to train as a counsellor and then as an executive coach. I learned that, while I'd had a good understanding of business, I'd been a mystery to myself. I was a hostage to my moods, my thoughts and my emotions and had become a walking example of self-sabotage. Not only that but while I was great at some elements of business, namely sales, marketing and innovation, I was rubbish at managing people, teams and processes.

I fell in love with the coaching profession when I discovered it in 1998. I loved how practical and applicable the concepts were, and the power that psychology had to enhance professional success. Here, laid out in front of me, were a simple set of steps to take to understand and manage myself: take care of x, y and z, and stay focused on a, b and c, and you'll be happy and successful. I felt like I'd discovered life's missing instruction manual.

I launched my coaching practice in 2001 to share these ideas with other founders and leaders so that they didn't need to blow up their businesses and lives the way I had. I've been refining, developing and delivering those ideas to founders ever since.

This is the book I needed when I was twenty-six. The ideas it contains have helped hundreds of my clients avoid the mistakes I made. More than that, it contains ideas that will enable you to be the most effective, successful and thriving founder you can be.

Are you ready for this book?

In my work as a coach, when I speak to a founder who's just won their first game-changing client or their first round of investment, most will assume their future is bright. They've done the tough bit. They've proved their concept, product or business model and the sky's the limit.

At this stage, the idea that they may not be the next Steve Jobs will be anathema to them. Founders with this mindset aren't ready to think about scaling their leadership or growing themselves, much as it would benefit them. I rarely take them on as clients.

If you're at this stage and you recognise yourself, this book is probably not for you right now. Maybe pick it up again in a year.

Let's jump forward twelve months to visit the founder who's in the early scale-up phase. The business now has a staff of between fifteen and one hundred people, as well as a wider range of clients, investors and stakeholders.

When I speak with scale-up founders, here are the kinds of things they tell me:

▸   I spend my entire time dealing with people problems.

▸   I can't believe people missed this/got this wrong/didn't do XYZ.

▸   My investors/board are a pain in the ass… they don't help, they just slow us down.

▸   I've hired managers/a COO/a head of people to do the people/management thing. Why aren't they dealing with this?

▸   I am exhausted.

Faced with these challenges, most founders double down on the things that helped them succeed in the start-up phase. They work harder and longer, they run from problem to problem fixing things, and they try to pitch people – their team, their investors – into submission.

Unfortunately, these solutions have themselves become problems. I let the founders know that they can't fix scale-up problems with start-up leadership. If they are open and motivated enough, these are the people who hire me and successfully scale themselves and their businesses.

If you recognise yourself here, this is the book for you. Welcome.

"

Very few founders survive the scale-up journey, let alone thrive during it, but it doesn't have to be that way.

You can grow your leadership and continue to drive your magic and talent into the business you founded. Both you and the business will benefit as a result.

How to use this book

To survive and thrive as a founder you need to be able to scale your leadership as you scale your business.

Scaling your leadership is about understanding what your business, people and stakeholders require of you at different stages of business growth and having the ability to adapt your leadership style and behaviours accordingly. To do this you need to understand three key concepts:

- Three modes of leadership
- Two styles of communication
- Two elements of self-mastery

The next chapter explores the different stages of business and what they require of you as a founder. We'll then move on to three parts, which tackle in turn the three key concepts you need to understand and master if your business is going to survive, thrive and grow.

Part One explores the three leadership modes your business will require of you and shows you how to either dial up or dial down each mode.

Part Two focuses on the two communication styles and how to Communicate to Manage and Communicate to Influence.

Part Three looks at the two elements of self-mastery, namely, Mind Mastery and Energy Mastery.

At the end of each chapter you will find a self-assessment and a guide telling you where to find relevant exercises and reading.

At the end of the book, the Toolbox provides you with key exercises relating to each chapter.

The book is designed to be used in different ways, depending on your preferences and current challenges. You can:

- ► Read Parts One to Three in their entirety, then dip into the section of the Toolbox that interests you.

- ► Skip straight to the section you know you need the most – leadership modes, communication skills or self-mastery.

- ► Take the self-assessments at the end of each chapter and focus on the chapters where you score lowest.

- ► Keep the book to hand and use it to find answers to specific challenges you face.

However you choose to use *The Founder's Survival Guide*, I wish you the greatest success. Founders are unique and brilliant, and the founder journey is a rollercoaster of exhilarating highs and crushing stresses. Go well on the adventure with my heartfelt admiration.

Think of these three elements – leadership modes, communication styles and self-mastery – as the three legs of your founder survival stool.

You need all three legs for the stool to be stable.

1

What Does Your Business Need From You?

My founder story is not unique. It may have involved more late nights and hardcore techno than most, but my trajectory from start-up success to scale-up failure is commonplace.

As many as four in five start-ups will fail in their first three years. Of those businesses that secure venture capital (VC), only one or two in ten will produce substantial returns. Even if a business makes it through these hurdles, the founder may not. Only 25% of companies holding an initial public offering retain their founder as CEO.[1]

Market trends, competition and failures of marketing, product and pricing all play a part in this picture, but up to a quarter of VC-backed start-ups fail for reasons of leadership.[2] The leaders burn out or lose focus, they don't attract and retain the right team, or they don't manage underperforming teams or disgruntled stakeholders.

A founder may not be able to change the market or the competition, but they can change their leadership and performance. Founders *can* scale their leadership as their business develops from start-up to scale-up to grown-up.

And it's worth it, for both the founder and the business. Having poured their heart and soul into their start-up, founders are devastated if they are shoved out to make way for 'a professional CEO'. Meanwhile, research suggests there

1   N Wasserman, 'The founder's dilemma', *Harvard Business Review* (February 2008), https://hbr.org/2008/02/the-founders-dilemma, accessed 8 April 2022
2   CB Insights, 'The top 12 reasons why startups fail', CB Insights (2019), www.cbinsights.com/research-12-reasons-why-startups-fail, accessed 8 April 2022

is both a performance and cultural benefit to the business of retaining founders as leaders.[3]

What does it take to be a successful founder of a growing business?

Let's imagine our founder as a professional tennis player who dreams of becoming Wimbledon champion. If they have a killer forehand shot, they may win a couple of games, but unless they also have a decent serve, they're not going to get far.

With a killer forehand and a decent serve, they might win more games, maybe even the odd local tournament. But to be a champion tennis player, they will need a serviceable backhand and to be able to lob and volley.

With a killer forehand, a decent serve, a serviceable backhand, lob and volley they will be a formidable player on the circuit. Their killer forehand may still be the strongest shot in their repertoire, but they now have a range of techniques they can call on as they face different opponents on their way to grand slam victory.

Most founders have a couple of killer shots in their arsenal. They are typically innovative, determined and convincing and will use these shots to try to win every match – whether they are the right shots or not. Whatever problems they or their business are facing, their tendency will be to come up with more new ideas, push and work even harder or convince others of their point of view.

Your killer shots are your greatest asset, but they become your greatest liability if they are all you have and you overuse them. As your business grows, you will need to have different techniques – different ways of leading, communicating and operating – if you are going to continue being an effective founder. If, like the pro-tennis player, you want to be a champion, you'll need to consider the match and player you

---

3   N Wasserman, 'The founder's dilemma'

are facing at any given time and adapt your play accordingly. You will use your killer shots whenever you possibly can, but if you need to play a backhand or lob you will be able to.

Champion tennis players depend on more than their shot repertoire to achieve success. They also know that the inner game is as important as the outer game. To win a championship, they need their head in the right place. They know that if they walk onto a court feeling doubtful and insecure, or if they lose their temper and throw their racket around, they will lose matches. They know that if they don't sleep or eat well, their performance will be hampered. Champion tennis players take great care of their physical, psychological and emotional needs to ensure they can show up to each tournament match-fit and formidable. Successful founders need to do the same.

In my work with founders, it's rare that I meet anyone who has all these bases covered. Even with founders who know how to play all the shots, their unmet psychological needs, beliefs or habits will often be the cause of self-sabotage. For some, it's the massive ego they needed to get the business off the ground that becomes their kryptonite as they scale. For others, it's the need for control or approval that trips them up. For still others, it's the ten shots of espresso followed by the bottle of wine. There's nothing inherently wrong with having a big ego, a need for approval or a caffeine habit, but if you want to successfully scale your business and still be part of the business once it's scaled, you'll likely need to master these things too.

What stage of growth is your business in?

Elizabeth was a firecracker digital media entrepreneur. She had a reputation for creating viral content and high-profile brands flocked to her for her digital media magic. She came to me when her latest venture was eighteen months old and she had seventeen members of staff. She told me it was the fourth business she had launched in the past decade. All her ventures had been incredibly successful for the first two years. She would come up with a great idea, convince amazing clients to buy into it, craft a brilliant brand, attract fabulous people to work with her and everything would be rosy.

'Then it all starts to crack,' she said. 'I get stressed, my team gets unhappy, mistakes start to happen in client delivery, and I decide to jack it all in and start something different. That was OK in my twenties, but I can't keep doing it forever.'

Martin set up his own software company and built it to a well-oiled machine of forty people within the first four years. Then the company secured a huge capital investment. Exponential growth followed and by the time he called me a year later, he had 400 employees and was on the verge of a nervous breakdown.

'I'm involved in every major decision,' he said. 'I can't be everything my investors need me to be, keep all my staff happy, make all these hiring decisions, dip down into crucial sales, manage operations, lead culture, track finances. I have a leadership team of eighteen people, but I seem to be the only one doing any leading.'

Elizabeth and Martin are examples of founders who excel at one stage of business, but flounder at the next. For Elizabeth the things that made her exceptional as a start-up entrepreneur were the kryptonite of her scale-up experience. For Martin, the style of leadership that allowed him to grow a successful operation of forty people simply crumbled under the demands of a company ten times the size.

To understand what your business needs from you as a founder, you must first understand the stage of growth your business is in, and the unique leadership needs of that stage. In the business literature and research there are many definitions of these stages, but for the sake of ease, let's boil these down to three:

1. Start-up
2. Scale-up
3. Grown-up

"

Founder survival is about understanding what your business needs from you at different stages of growth, and having the ability to adapt your leadership accordingly.

"

You can't easily define these stages by organisational age, turnover or even staff numbers. Many of those characteristics are determined by your business model and approach to funding. Broadly, though, we can define each stage as follows:

Start-up

- You have one team.
- You directly manage almost everyone in the organisation.
- You are involved in almost all decisions.
- You are making some money.
- You are bootstrapping early growth or working with early seed capital.
- Your priorities are product/service development, sales and investment.

Scale-up

- You employ more people than can sit around a dining room table.
- You have functional managers who are responsible for key duties and manage sub-teams.
- You are no longer involved in every decision and don't know everything that's happening.
- You are experiencing significant year-on-year growth in turnover.
- You are funding growth through VC investment or by reinvesting profits.
- Your priorities are funding growth, attracting talent, delegation and improving effectiveness.

Grown-up

- You employ hundreds of people, often in multiple locations.
- You have, or need, a management structure that can sustain growth.

- You depend on an executive team and senior leaders to run most of the business.

- You have, or need, extensive and well-developed systems.

- You likely have a governance structure or board of directors.

- Your priorities are keeping up with competition, innovation and market changes, organisational health and culture, and growing organisational value.

What your business needs from you at different stages of growth

Depending on the stage of business you are at, or the challenge you are facing, your business may require very different things from you as a leader. For example:

At the start-up stage your business needs you to:	At the scale-up stage your business needs you to:	At the grown-up stage your business needs you to:
Be single-minded in pursuit of a goal	Be thoughtful about people and process	Be the inspiring figurehead
Have bulletproof personal confidence	Have a high degree of emotional intelligence	Have enormous gravitas and presence
Be a brilliant tactician	Be a brilliant systems thinker	Be a brilliant strategist
Convince people in one-to-one pitches	Build consensus and high performance in your team	Inspire/reassure large groups of stakeholders
Have lots of ideas and be able to flex between them	Assess and implement a few great ideas	Identify and implement one or two game-changing strategic ideas

Obviously, this is oversimplified. There may be times during start-up when you need to inspire large groups, and there may be times in a grown-up business when you need to be a brilliant tactician. As a founder, you need to be able to cycle between these different ways of thinking and behaving on a regular basis. That's not easy, and no founder I have ever worked with is brilliant at all of them.

Of course, you'll build a team, delegate, and aim to play from your strengths and preferences, but you will still need to develop adaptable leadership skills and know when to deploy them. You'll need to know when to focus on new ideas and inspiring people and when to help your team focus on the considered implementation of a plan. You'll need to know when to jump in and fix a problem yourself and when to pull back and let your team take ownership. To do that effectively, you will need the self-awareness to know when a leadership strength has become a vulnerability, and when to adapt your style to the challenge you're facing.

This is all beginning to sound a bit difficult, isn't it? It's simpler than it sounds – simple, but not easy. It requires determination, humility and bravery. But the alternatives are much worse. No founder wants their business to fail. Nor do they want to stunt the growth of their business, and they certainly don't want to be forced out of the business they launched.

If you want to give your business the best chance of not just surviving but thriving, and if you want to be there to see it thrive, you must scale your leadership. Part One shows you where to begin.

PART ONE

THE THREE LEADERSHIP MODES

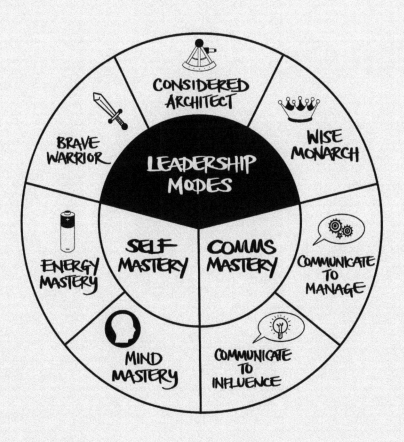

An Introduction To Leadership Modes

Bob graduated with a First in Computer Science from Oxford University. In his mid-thirties, he saw an opportunity in the AI space, developed his own proprietary software and left corporate life to launch his software firm. He was extremely driven, technically brilliant and an inspiring communicator. Within two years, he had a small team of committed staff and investors clamouring to fund a high-potential scale-up. Everyone was talking 10x growth and Bob was flying high.

A year after taking significant capital investment the cracks started to appear. As staff numbers tripled, rumblings of employee discontent could be heard around the water coolers and on Slack. Leadership team meetings became increasingly fractious and two key members of staff resigned. Investors started to question Bob's leadership capability and board meetings became a source of dread.

When one of Bob's investors suggested he get a coach to help him with his leadership, he was offended. 'I don't need help with my leadership,' he said. 'I just think my team need to get on with the job I've hired them to do.'

As part of Bob's coaching programme, I interviewed some of his team, investors and clients to understand their experience of Bob's leadership. Everyone admired his vision, his commitment, his passion and his dedication. No one worked as hard as Bob. No one knew more about AI than Bob. Any technical problem the leadership team had, Bob knew the solution.

But Bob was a hammer, and any problem he found, he hammered it. When he saw something that wasn't perfect, he jumped on it. If anyone underperformed, he grabbed the task and did it himself. If any member of the board didn't agree with him, he'd argue and shout until he got what he wanted. One of his team described his leadership style as 'The Eye of Sauron' and they spent their time hoping that the Eye was on someone else this week.

No one knew where they stood. 'We have this grand vision,' said one of his leadership team, 'but absolutely no plan, no clear roles, no milestones. Bob cancels our management meetings most weeks, so I've no idea what he or anyone else is working on.'

Bob spent his time moving from one breaking project to another. One week he'd dive down into the development team, changing code, ripping up their plan, arguing that their direction was completely wrong. They'd change their plans and workflow and get ready to present back to him the following week. In the meantime, he'd move on to fix a burning problem in the sales team, so when it came to the scheduled meeting to review the development team's plans, he'd tell the CTO, 'I don't have time to review that now – just do whatever you think.'

Bob's leadership team tried to tell him that they needed a clear plan and that he needed to delegate more effectively, but nothing they said seemed to make any difference. Bob became super-defensive, doubled down on his natural leadership mode and grew increasingly resentful of his 'whinging staff'. This, of course, exacerbated the problem.

The investors were no happier. Bob would come to regular board meetings and announce a complete change in direction or a new idea he'd come up with. When the board challenged him, Bob would try to talk them into submission, reverting to his 'inspirational-pitch' mode, or he would try to bamboozle them with his technical wizardry. If pushed, he got aggressive, blaming team members, customers or investors for problems. Investors didn't feel heard or reassured, and increasingly questions were being asked about whether Bob had what it took to lead the business through the planned scale-up.

'I think I'm a good leader,' said Bob in one of our first sessions. 'If I wasn't, how could I have raised so much capital from investors and attracted so much top talent to come and work for me?'

Bob was right. He was a good leader – for the start-up phase of the business. But he hadn't scaled his leadership as the business scaled. Now the very strengths that had made him great at the start-up phase were proving to be the kryptonite of the scale-up phase. Bob had one way to lead, and even though it was no longer working, he didn't know how else to do it. So he kept doubling down on what he knew – in effect, doubling the kryptonite.

The WAM model

Most founders don't spend a lot of time thinking about their leadership, they simply do 'what comes naturally'. Or they assume that who they are is how they lead and can't be changed. Like Bob, when faced with problems, they do more of what's worked in the past, then get frustrated and impatient if that doesn't work.

Successful founders know that being able to adapt and flex their leadership is essential. They understand that what their team, customers and investors need from them changes radically as the business grows.

When I start working with a founder, we reflect on their leadership and the challenges they face in their business and explore the link between the two. Then we explore how they can adapt their style to meet the evolving needs of the business while remaining authentic and true to themselves.

To help my clients navigate these complexities, I created the WAM model, which refers to three key leadership modes founders need to develop as they scale their business. These are:

1. The Brave **W**arrior

2. The Considered **A**rchitect

3. The Wise **M**onarch

These three styles correlate to three different stages of business growth.

The WAM Model		
Leadership mode	**Business stage**	**Leadership characteristics**
Brave Warrior	Start-up	Single-minded, bullet-proof self-belief, fast and full of ideas
Considered Architect	Scale-up	Team/systems thinker, calm and unflappable, expert planner
Wise Monarch	Grown-up	Strategist, gravitas and presence, politically astute

I use the WAM model and these three archetypes as easy touchstones to help clients remember how they need to show up at different stages of their business.

Pause for a moment and think about a Brave Warrior. See them charging on the field of battle – fearless, focused, determined, adaptable. They find a way around any obstacle, ignore the injury to their leg, roar at their troops to follow them once more into the breach. They are single-minded, bulletproof, fast, innovative, adaptable and comfortable with risk. You need all of these attributes at the start-up phase of your business.

Now imagine a Considered Architect poring over blueprints at head office. They're wondering how to build the skyscraper, how much glass and steel they'll need, what will need to happen first, second, third, fourth. They're pondering the teams they'll need, and the systems they'll put in place. They are planning and systematising and, once the build commences, they're on site talking to their teams, solving problems and keeping the plan on track. You need to be able to do all of these things at the scale-up phase of your business.

"

Most founders don't spend a lot of time thinking about their leadership. They do more of what's worked in the past, then get frustrated when that doesn't work.

And last but not least think of the Wise Monarch. Imagine them walking into their court, oozing gravitas and authority. See how they hold themselves tall, how unflappable and calm they look. See them conversing with their courtiers, greeting the public with a smile and a question. In moments of adversity they are either reassuring or rallying their people. In ancient times the Wise Monarch was the chief diplomat, strategist and figurehead, the person we trusted and wanted to follow. You need to be all of these things at the grown-up phase of your business.

Adapting leadership modes to business stage or challenge

To explain how these three leadership modes work at different stages of business growth, let's take the example of a successful warrior king, William the Conqueror, who invaded England in 1066 and reigned until his death:

▶ He started in Brave Warrior mode, winning the battle of Hastings (start-up).

▶ He quickly leaned into Considered Architect mode and built a peaceful and successful kingdom. He focused on building fortifications all over the south-east of England and co-opted local barons and leaders to his side, the mediaeval version of systems and a leadership team (scale-up).

▶ Once his new territory was established, he moved to Wise Monarch mode, focused his energy on managing threats and opportunities abroad, and ensured continued followership at home, think strategy, politics and gravitas (grown-up).

Apologies to any historians out there – I know this is hugely oversimplified, but it illustrates the point.

It's not just your stage of business growth, however, that will inform the leadership mode you need to lean into. There are challenges you will face at each stage that will be better addressed if you can adapt your leadership mode accordingly. There are times during the start-up phase where you'll need the strategic thinking of the Wise Monarch. There are times during scale-up where you'll need to access your Brave Warrior so you can drive immediate change. There are times during the grown-up stage where you'll need to channel your Considered Architect to ensure your top team is functioning well and with strong operational grip.

Mode	Most helpful when you need to
Brave Warrior	Make decisions fast, drive immediate forceful action, win business/investment
Considered Architect	Solve problems at source, build a high-performance team, design systems
Wise Monarch	Think big-picture strategy, rally the troops or stakeholders

None of these leadership modes is right or wrong, they are simply right or wrong for a specific challenge. Your ability to lean into each mode, while playing to your natural strengths, will dictate how successful you are at stewarding your business through the different stages and challenges of business growth.

Most founders I work with exhibit some characteristics of each leadership mode, but most have a preferred mode they default to. Similarly, most have one mode they find most difficult to employ, regardless of the needs of the business.

If you've picked up this book it's likely that you are facing some challenges in your founder journey. I'd be happy to bet that a lot of those challenges are happening because you're using the wrong leadership mode in any given situation. You're warrior-ing when you need to be architect-ing, architect-ing when you need to be monarch-ing, or monarch-ing... well, you get the idea.

"

Warriors keep warrior-ing when they need to architect a plan.

Architects keep architect-ing when their business needs visionary leadership.

Monarchs keep monarch-ing when the business needs organisational grip.

"

In the next three chapters, we'll explore each of these modes in more detail, look at how each plays at different stages of business growth and when to dial them up or down. At the end of each chapter, there are self-assessments to help you identify which is your strongest and weakest mode. You'll also find a brief guide pointing to exercises in the Toolbox and chapters in the book that will help you dial up or dial down that specific leadership mode. I recommend you read all three chapters first, then decide where to focus your energy.

Before we begin, I want to address two objections founders often have to adapting their leadership mode.

Objection 1: 'I am who I am, and I can't change.'

Sometimes leaders are resistant to the idea of developing themselves or evolving their leadership. They say things like, 'Entrepreneurs/Managers/Leaders are born, not made,' or, 'It would be inauthentic to adapt my style.'

The reality is that, after 100 years of research, psychologists still can't agree on how much human behaviour is fixed and moveable, how much is nature and how much nurture. In the meantime, business psychologists and writers propose *both* playing to your strengths *and* flexing your leadership style to the challenge you're facing.

Daniel Goleman, of *Emotional Intelligence* fame, researched the impact of different leadership styles on the performance of organisations. In his 2000 *Harvard Business Review* article 'Leadership that gets results', he identified six different leadership styles – coercive, authoritative, affiliative, democratic, pacesetting and coaching – and correlated leadership style with organisational performance. He found that the leaders who generated the best results didn't rely on one style of leadership. In fact, they used multiple styles depending on the business situation.[4]

---

4   D Goleman, 'Leadership that gets results', *Harvard Business Review* (March–April 2000), https://hbr.org/2000/03/leadership-that-gets-results, accessed 12 April 2022

Often leaders with one fixed and preferred leadership style aren't able to give their team or their organisation what they need on any given day. The founders who achieve the most astonishing results are those who both honour their preferred mode in their choice of role and focus, and have the ability to dial each of these modes up or down as the business demands.

Let's take two people who want to play sport. One is 7'7", the other is 5'2". The taller individual is best suited to basketball and the shorter person would make a better jockey. But they can both learn to ride a horse, and they can both learn to shoot a hoop. At certain times, your business is going to require you to shoot hoops, and at others, you'll need to get in the saddle. If you don't learn how to do both, you are going to let the business down.

Objection 2: 'I don't need to adapt my leadership, I'm delegating the bits I'm no good at.'

Of course, a team is strong if the tall people are playing basketball, and the short people are racing horses. Likewise, you want your warriors selling, your architects managing and your monarchs strategising and inspiring. But unless you are aware of your default mode and its impact on your people and your team, you will undo most, if not all, the good work your team is trying to do. You'll hire great architects, then burn through their meetings and their work like a tornado of warrior energy, or you'll abdicate rather than delegate, because you're having too much fun playing the visionary monarch.

If you are a super-strong Brave Warrior or a natural Wise Monarch, you will be best off hiring a stellar COO fast – or at least an incredibly efficient assistant, project manager or second-in-command. *And* you need to develop enough Considered Architect energy to manage them effectively.

Now we've put these objections aside, it's time to find out more about each leadership mode.

2

The Brave Warrior Mode

We all know what we mean when we say the word 'warrior'. Whether you are in a Papua New Guinean tribe, on a rugby pitch or on Wall Street, the warrior is an archetype that crosses time, culture and context.

The Brave Warrior is single-minded, brave and driven in pursuit of a win. Drop a Brave Warrior on a beach and tell them to take the gun turret and they will do it or die trying. That gun turret is all the warrior sees, getting to it is all the warrior cares about. Even if a fellow falls, the warrior keeps going. Shrapnel hits their leg; they wrap a tourniquet around it and charge ahead. The path is blocked; the warrior finds another way. Their weapon jams; they find another one. The plan falls apart; the warrior thinks on their feet and keeps going. The *only* thing that matters to the warrior is winning. And win they often do.

Brave Warriors are awe-inspiring. Others are swept up in their courage and confidence. When we are flailing around and don't know what to do, we love their certainty and determination. In a crisis, it's great to have someone who seems to know what they're doing and doesn't seem afraid. Hell yeah, we'll join in their war cry and follow them into battle!

Brave Warriors love the battlefield – whether that's a beach in some far-flung military campaign or a boardroom in Palo Alto. They are less sure of themselves when there is no fight to be won, which is why they often pick one. The Brave Warrior is all about triumphing over adversity, beating the odds, achieving that specific goal, climbing that peak. When the fight is over, it can feel anticlimactic. Without that single all-encompassing focus, they feel lost, so they pick another battle and start again.

The Brave Warrior in business

Brave Warriors in business are single-minded, goal-oriented and driven. They are courageous, comfortable with risk and will go to any lengths to win. They appear confident and self-assured, though they may not always feel that way. They are brilliant tacticians, innovators and problem-solvers. They love starting businesses.

The Brave Warrior in business	
How to spot them	▸ Single-minded ▸ Bullet-proof self-belief ▸ Fast and full of ideas ▸ Can be intolerant and impatient ▸ Fond of caffeine, alcohol or adrenaline
Most helpful for	▸ Driving fast change ▸ Responding to a crisis ▸ Meeting a deadline ▸ Generating immediate output or results ▸ Starting new initiatives ▸ Winning business ▸ Selling or pitching
On a good day	An animated force of nature who can shift immovable obstacles at speed
On a bad day	A monomaniacal egotist who tears through the business like a tornado
Stage of business	Launch and start-up

A word on gender: as a proud recovering female warrior myself, I've never thought that the warrior mode was 'male'; however, I know some people may read this as a 'male' word. In this chapter I've referred to warriors using the nongendered them/they/their, but if the word 'warrior' feels too gendered I encourage you to think Boudica or Joan of Arc. Or, if you like your references more twenty-first-century, think Emily Blunt in Edge of Tomorrow.

The Brave Warrior is single-minded, brave and driven in pursuit of the win.

Your Brave Warrior mode is brilliant for the start-up stage, but becomes more destructive as the business scales.

The Brave Warrior is your typical start-up entrepreneur. They have a goal and nothing is going to get in their way. No money – they'll get it. No time – they'll find it. No network – they'll make it. **The Brave Warrior is single-minded in pursuit of a business goal**, and nothing will stop them.

They have incredible amounts of energy and a prodigious work capacity. If you need a fifty-page analysis done right now, ask a Brave Warrior – they'll work all night to get it done. You'll be astounded by how much work the Warrior can churn through, and it will be impressive work too.

The Brave Warrior in business has stores of tenacity and resilience others can only dream of (seemingly, at least). They will keep pitching and pitching and pitching and, even when they get ninety-nine rejections, they'll strap on their self-belief and a winning smile, pitch for the hundredth time, and win that one. Their confidence and self-belief seem unshakeable. When they're at home alone after the ninety-ninth defeat, staring into their whiskey glass, they will have a dark night of the soul, but they won't show you this.

The Brave Warrior in business is comfortable with lightning-fast change. That pitch didn't land – adapt it. That client wants it with tubular bells and gold leaf – no problem. That investor didn't like the idea for off-shoring customer service – they'll on-shore it. Fast changes to ensure a win – they come up with them, no problem at all. **Conversely, they can be incredibly resistant to change if they think it's someone else's idea**, or if they think someone is suggesting they are wrong – that's just another battle they'll try to win.

They are brilliant tactical thinkers and problem-solvers. The Brave Warrior will find a way through, around or over any objection. As a result, they tend to be **full of innovative ideas, fixes and solutions.** This is great at the start-up phase, but at the scale-up phase can cause whiplash for the rest of the team, who thought they were doing [x] on Monday and found out on Tuesday that they're doing [y] instead; or when they discover the warrior has promised a client tubular bells with gold leaf, when they thought they were selling banana bread and muffins.

The Brave Warrior in business is comfortable with ambiguity and risk. They'll say yes today and work out the rest tomorrow. They know they'll find a way, even if it's not clear right now. Their complete belief in their idea and themselves means they have a lower need for the clarity, certainty and stability their team may need.

The Brave Warrior needs freedom and autonomy. Give them a laptop and freedom and they'll take over the world, but they'll buck against anything which feels like a restriction. If they're expected to abide by a protocol or show up to a daily team huddle they'll be inwardly rolling their eyes and full of resentment – or they'll just cancel it.

The Brave Warrior in business can be incredibly compelling. Their fierce belief in their idea or business can be magnetic; it can pull people, customers and investors into their orbit. Their force of will can be irresistible. Their willingness to go to any lengths to win the deal/pitch/investment pays off. Delivering on those promises, can sometimes be a different story.

The Brave Warrior gets power by taking action. They don't wait to be asked or given permission. They don't wait until the team are happy or the board approves – they act first and work the rest out later. Their motto is likely, 'It's better to ask for forgiveness than permission.'

They have a strong 'Hurry up, let's get it done!' driver. They can be impatient and intolerant of anything that they perceive as slowing them down or wasting time. Long, drawn-out team discussions drive them crazy. Pausing to update their team or to think through the ramifications of their actions is not their strongest suit.

The Brave Warrior mode and stages of business

The Brave Warrior at the start-up phase

Most founders I coach are natural Brave Warriors and, if you're reading this book, the likelihood is that you score high on the Brave Warrior mode too. That, of course, is because the Brave Warrior makes an ideal start-up entrepreneur.

The start-up phase of a business requires:

▶ A big idea – an opportunity or need that your start-up is going to tap into

▶ A proof of concept – the way you turn this idea into a profitable product/business

▶ Money – either initial customers or investors

It requires a founder who:

▶ Is completely goal-focused, and never takes their eyes off the prize

▶ Can flip between a 100,000-foot view (the big idea) and the 10-foot view (the next step)

▶ Has bulletproof belief in themselves and their idea, to survive the endless rounds of pitching and rejection

▶ Is mono-maniacal about proof of concept, product–market fit and generating money – without these, the game's over

The Brave Warrior mode is uniquely powerful for you at the start-up phase. When acting from your Brave Warrior mode:

▶ Your risk tolerance means you can traverse an uncertain start-up world with ease.

▶ Your self-belief and desire to win make you compelling in pitch conversations, and good at convincing investors and customers to buy into your ideas.

- Your comfort with ambiguity, speed and new ideas are beneficial at a stage in business that will require you to evolve, innovate and iterate every day.

- Your enormous energy and single-mindedness provide the rocket fuel your start-up needs to achieve lift-off.

The Brave Warrior at the scale-up phase

Brave Warriors tend to be really successful at the start-up phase. Then what?

As the business grows to the scale-up phase – where they can no longer fit all their team members around a dining room table, all their customers on a single spreadsheet, all their systems on the back of a napkin – the Brave Warrior can come unstuck fast.

The scale-up phase requires founders to lean into systems and processes, to focus on people development, to build and implement the plan for growth. In these endeavours, the very things that made the Brave Warrior so successful in the start-up phase become weaknesses:

- Their speed, constant flow of new ideas and ability to change on a dime all confuse the people back at the office.

- Their 'Hurry up, let's get it done!' driver starts to burn their people out and disrupt the systems and processes the team depends on.

- Their comfort with ambiguity means they are less likely to provide their team with the clarity they need (about roles, the plan, etc).

- They're so used to selling and convincing that they struggle with the fine art of engaging teams and creating the buy-in and collaboration that a scale-up needs to succeed.

If you are a Brave Warrior leading a scale-up, it really hurts.

CASE STUDY: JAMES

James was a natural Brave Warrior entrepreneur who started coaching with me when his team had grown to about twenty-five people and the cracks were beginning to show. Classic scale-up problems abounded. James spent an inordinate amount of time refereeing disagreements between members of his team, feeling frustrated by poor performance, and managing complaints from customers. 'No one would ever call me the most sensitive people manager,' he said, 'but I don't want to spend my life managing people and teams. I just want all the problems to stop.'

The first thing we looked at together was how James could provide 'minimally viable people and process management', just enough to give his people what they needed to thrive and free him up to do the things he loved to do (sell, innovate, raise money).

We started by helping James pause before leaping into action. He had a tendency, like many Brave Warriors, to speak or act first and think later. This caused huge problems for his team, as he promised things to clients that the team couldn't deliver, or announced new business ideas that confused people. We introduced two new phrases to his management repertoire: 'Let me speak to my team and get back to you' for use with clients and 'How do you think we should solve that?' for use with his team.

These two phrases inserted a pause before action and gave him enough time to think through implications before making decisions. It also helped his team feel more responsible for solving their own problems, and meant they felt both heard and engaged.

James noticed it was much easier to use these phrases on some days than others. On days when he was tired, hungover, angry or resentful, he reverted straight back to Brave Warrior mode and things went off-piste quickly. We looked at mind management techniques to help him feel less triggered, and at energy management to ensure he felt less tired and grumpy. (See Part Three for more on this.)

Finally, James needed to manage his focus. He often had fifteen brilliant new ideas before breakfast, most of which he'd share with his team as soon as they crossed his mind. James hired a chief of staff and we worked together to create a cadence of management meetings to ensure annual and quarterly priorities, goals and milestones were set in a more structured way. The chief of staff set up project management software which allowed James and his team to track progress against these goals. James, in the meantime, tried hard not to introduce new ideas outside of these standard meetings. The breakthrough came when we introduced the idea of an 'Ideas Reserve' folder. Whenever James had a new idea he added it to the folder and he'd review them in our coaching sessions to see which ideas needed to be acted on immediately, and which could wait until the next monthly management or quarterly planning session.

Within six months, James reported a radical reduction in the fires he had to fight. The team were clearer on what they needed to do and solved more problems for themselves, while client complaints had reduced significantly as James stopped overpromising. James had more time and space to think about the big-picture ideas that could elevate the business. 'I can't say I enjoy the management meetings,' he said. 'But beforehand, I spent about 80% of my time solving people problems, and now I spend 10% of my time in meetings giving people what they need so that those problems don't exist. That's a deal I'm happy to take.'

The Brave Warrior on a good day: an animated force of nature who can shift immovable obstacles at speed.

The Brave Warrior on a bad day: a monomaniacal egotist who tears through the business like a tornado.

Dial up or dial down your Brave Warrior mode

You may immediately recognise yourself in this chapter and think, 'Yep, that's me. Brave Warrior through and through.' Or you may not be sure if Brave Warrior is your default leadership mode. If that's the case, there's a self-test at the end of this chapter to help you find out. Whether it's your default or not, there are times when your business will need you to dial up or dial down your Brave Warrior mode and it's helpful to know when those are.

When you're pitching or innovating, when you're responding to an urgent deadline or need to complete work fast, the Brave Warrior mode is your friend. But when you're managing people and performance, or implementing systems and a plan, you will need to dial it down. Likewise, when you need to show up with poise, or work on culture and strategy, you'll find it helpful to dial down your Brave Warrior mode.

Dial up your Brave Warrior when:	Dial down your Brave Warrior when:
Pitching	Managing people – an individual, a team or stakeholders
Coming up with new, disruptive ideas	Implementing systems, a roadmap or plan
Working alone	Managing performance and giving feedback
Tasks need completing fast	Working on culture and organisational health
There is urgent work that only you can do	Engaging or inspiring large groups of people
You need to feel pumped-up	You need to feel calm and considered

What next?

Complete the Brave Warrior self-test at the end of this chapter, then ask yourself 'Given the challenges we're facing and our stage of business, do I need to dial up or dial down my Brave Warrior mode?'

If you need to dial up, focus on the Brave Warrior exercises in the Toolbox. The Brave Warrior is all about single-minded pursuit of a specific goal, and any exercise that connects you with a vision of the future that excites and inspires you will increase your Brave Warrior energy. In the Toolbox you'll find exercises to connect you with a vision, dial up your self-belief and pump up your energy and inspiration.

As a founder, though, it's more likely that you already score high on the Brave Warrior mode and will need to learn to dial it down a bit. If that's the case, read the section on self-mastery first (Part Three) because unless you're able to manage your mind and your energy you will find it difficult to do so.

Once you've done that:

▸ If you need to dial down to effectively manage people, performance, systems and plans, read Chapter 3 (The Considered Architect Mode) and Chapter 5 (Communicate to Manage)

▸ If you need to dial down to work on culture or strategy, or to engage and inspire large groups of people, read Chapter 4 (The Wise Monarch Mode) or Chapter 6 (Communicate to Influence).

Brave Warrior self-test	0 Very rarely	1 Rarely	2 Often	3 Very often
I am single-minded in pursuit of a goal				
I am self-confident				
I work fast				
I am full of ideas				
I make decisions quickly				
I like to take action				
I respond best if people are quick and to the point				
I am good at pitching				
I am good in a crisis				
I work harder than most people I know				
I start new initiatives				
I have lots of ideas and I'm highly innovative				
I'm good at winning business and selling				
I am comfortable with fast change				
I am tenacious				
I have a prodigious work capacity				
I am good at solving problems				
I am comfortable with ambiguity and risk				
I work best when I have autonomy				
People tell me I am compelling				

Brave Warrior self-test	0 Very rarely	1 Rarely	2 Often	3 Very often
I am known for taking action first, asking questions later				
I'd rather be fast than perfect				
I focus on what's next				
I am passionate				
I focus on winning business/ investment				
Column totals: (Score 1 for rarely, 2 for often and 3 for very often)				
Add your column scores together to give you your **Brave Warrior score:**				

Your Brave Warrior score

If you scored 60–75: Congratulations, you are a Brave Warrior. If you are at the start-up stage of business, enjoy yourself. If you are at the scale-up or grown-up stage, you may need to dial up your Considered Architect or Wise Monarch modes. See the relevant sections of the Toolbox at the back of the book for how to do this.

If you scored 40–59: You can dial up your Brave Warrior mode when needed. If you feel you need to dial it up more right now, look at the exercises in the Brave Warrior Toolbox.

If you scored 0–39: You are low on natural Brave Warrior mode. Prioritise the exercises in the Brave Warrior Toolbox, particularly if your business is at the start-up phase.

3

The Considered Architect Mode

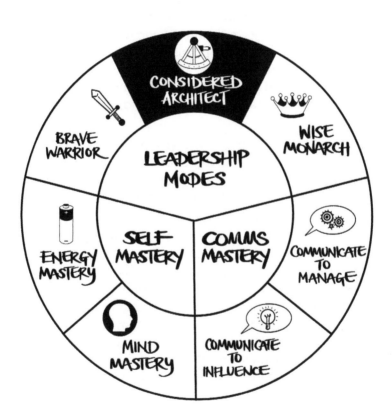

While the Brave Warrior is charging at their adversary on the field of battle, the Considered Architect is at headquarters poring thoughtfully over blueprints and plans.

Tell a Considered Architect you want to build a record-breaking skyscraper and they'll show you how to build it. They are geniuses at translating a vision into a set of blueprints, roadmaps, processes and systems. They can work out how many people will need to be on site and when. They will think through the timeline, who needs to do what and where the interdependencies and risks are. Once construction starts, the architect is on site, ensuring each team member is clear on their role, managing deadlines and dealing with any challenges.

Considered Architects are a pleasure to work with. They are calm, considered and dependable. We appreciate their unflappability and we relax knowing that they have a plan, will keep people on track and will ensure the build runs smoothly.

They love a system and a process. They are less sure of themselves when they need to act fast, innovate or inspire. They can get lost in the detail of the plans they are drawing, without realising that the investors, market or opportunity have shifted. They can build a beautiful skyscraper office block, only to realise that no one needed that much office space in the first place. Under pressure, they can double down on plans and details while a boatload of cash rolls straight past their door, or their high-performing team jumps ship to a more exciting and innovative project down the road.

"

The Considered Architect is a calm planner, thoughtful designer and genius systems thinker.

Your Considered Architect mode is worth its weight in gold during scale-up, but can fail to provide the visionary leadership a grown-up business requires.

"

The Considered Architect in business

The Considered Architect in business is a calm, thoughtful planner and genius systems thinker. They think before they speak, pause before acting and consider their impact on others. They know what their people need to be successful and make sure they provide that. They are brilliant managers and operations directors. They are worth their weight in gold at the scale-up stage of business.

The Considered Architect in business	
How to spot them	► Team and/or systems thinkers ► Calm and unflappable ► Think before they speak ► Love a plan/roadmap/Gantt chart ► Can appear distant or unemotional
Most helpful for	► Replacing chaos with clarity and consistency ► Developing a high-performing team ► Managing and coaching people ► Building systems and processes to enable fast growth ► Turning strategy into an implementable roadmap
On a good day	A thoughtful and emotionally intelligent leader with great operational grip and a happy and effective team
On a bad day	A micromanaging slowcoach who is so busy planning, they miss the big opportunity
Stage of business	Scale-up

While the Brave Warrior leader jumps straight into action and takes on every challenge for themselves, **the Considered Architect is a design-thinker, focused on the processes and systems a business and its people need to thrive.**

The Considered Architect in business creates order out of chaos. Give a Considered Architect a month and they will develop a clear roadmap and a set of priorities that everyone is aligned around.

They craft clarity and keep people focused. Their people know what their roles are, what the plan is, what the channels of communication are, where to go when they have a problem, and what their milestones and success metrics are.

The Considered Architect introduces ideas and implements change in a calm and organised manner. While Brave Warriors can suggest fifteen new ideas before breakfast, the Considered Architect knows that this can confuse people and take a team off track. They sound people out before they suggest new ideas and typically introduce a couple of key initiatives each quarter, often as part of the standard business planning and goal setting process that they've introduced.

The Considered Architect manages and mitigates risk. They think about what could take the system, plan or people off course. They hardwire processes into the business to review, plan and communicate work so that people are less likely to get a nasty surprise or run out of a vital component just before that huge delivery is due.

The Considered Architect thinks before they speak and reflects on the impact of their actions. While the Brave Warrior dives into action, the Considered Architect pauses. They are aware that their words and actions have the potential to help or hinder an entire ecosystem.

They understand what people need to be high-performing, and they hire, retain and enable talent. They assume nothing. They drive for clarity. They manage expectations. They provide milestones. They create accountability. They coach. While the Warrior sells and the Monarch inspires, the Architect elicits high performance from the people who work for them.

They manage their emotions, rather than managing *from* their emotions. The very fact that they are 'Considered' means they are less likely to act when agitated or triggered.

Considered Architects don't explode when angry or excited. They know how damaging this can be on individual and team performance. They might talk about emotions, but they rarely act or speak based on them.

The Considered Architect is consistent. They do what they say they'll do when they say they'll do it. They have balanced energy and are unlikely to blow hot and cold. You know where you stand with them.

The Considered Architect's authority is held. While the Warrior is busy jumping into action, the Architect crafts a plan, ensures people buy into it, then manages the implementation of that plan. The Considered Architect holds authority because people trust them and believe in the plan.

They have a strong 'Do it properly' driver. They can get stressed if the goalposts are constantly changing, or if you throw things into the mix that will upset the team or the plan. Fast, ill-thought-through change drives them crazy.

The Considered Architect mode and stages of business

The Considered Architect mode at the scale-up stage

Whether you are blitz-scaling your business with a bucketload of VC cash or bootstrapping gradual business growth, the moment you employ more people than can sit around a dining room table and/or more customers than you can manage personally, you are at the scale-up stage of business.

This is the stage where your brilliant start-up business idea gets translated into a set of processes, systems and ways of working that allow your business to scale. Often called the 'rattling rocket ship' phase, this can be the most profoundly uncomfortable and difficult stage for the founder. After the highs and wins of start-up, scale-up can feel like a constant round of problems, breakdowns, firefighting, infighting and stress. Things break, people leave, systems fail, customers complain, and the rocket rattles so much, you're not sure if it's going to make it out of the atmosphere.

At this stage of the business if you keep warrior-ing 24/7 you'll do untold damage to your business before it even has a chance to get into orbit. This is when you need to develop your Considered Architect leadership mode.

In this stage of growth your business needs:

▸ Well-managed, talented people

▸ Strong strategic planning

▸ Systems and processes

Even if your first hire is a stellar COO, the scale-up phase of a business requires you, as a founder, to:

▸ Delegate effectively

▸ Work collaboratively with your top team

▸ Co-create and then stick to a clear roadmap

▸ Hold people accountable and drive high performance

▸ Maintain strong operational grip

The Considered Architect mode is uniquely valuable to you at the scale-up stage. When acting from your Considered Architect mode:

▸ Your design thinking enables you to see the business as a set of systems that need to be engineered.

▸ Your calm unflappability enables you to provide the kind of leadership that your growing team needs.

▸ Your drive for clarity and consistency means that your growing tribe of people know what their roles are, what's expected of them and what they need to do to succeed.

▸ Your systems mindset ensures that you solve problems at their core, rather than running around fighting fires.

▸ Your considered approach to introducing new ideas and change means that your people stay pointed in the right direction, not following you as you chase shiny bright objects.

> The Considered Architect on a good day: a thoughtful and emotionally intelligent leader with great operational grip and a happy and effective team.
>
> The Considered Architect on a bad day: a micro-managing slow-coach who is so busy planning, they miss the big opportunity.

Considered Architects at the grown-up stage

Considered Architects are worth their weight in gold at the scale-up stage. Then what?

As the business shifts from scale-up to grown-up – when systems and processes are well established and departmental or functional heads are brought in to manage different parts of the business – the Considered Architect can come unstuck fast.

The grown-up phase of business requires a founder who focuses on big-picture strategy, the 100,000-foot view, organisational culture and innovation, reputation management, and inspiring/reassuring multiple sets of diverse stakeholders. The very things that made the Considered Architect so successful in the scale-up stage become the kryptonite of the grown-up stage:

▸ Their focus on operations means they fail to take the 100,000-foot view.

▸ Their operational grip becomes a stranglehold and undermines the top talent they've brought in to actually run the business.

▸ They are so busy checking the Gantt chart that they fail to look up and out, at their stakeholders, their competitors and the changing market.

▸ They fail to provide the inspirational and visible leadership that their employees and stakeholders need.

▸ They struggle to translate their high-performance team management skills into a high-performance organisational culture.

As a Considered Architect leading a grown-up business, your tried and tested tactics of operational leadership are probably not cutting it, and you'll feel that. You know you need to do something different, but you don't know what or how.

CASE STUDY: BRYONY

Bryony needed to dial up her Considered Architect mode. She hired me four years after launching a successful wealth management firm, feeling tired, overwhelmed and ineffective. 'I'm working eighteen hours a day,' she said. 'I have a lovely team of people and wonderful clients, but I don't have time to give them all what they need. I've hired an operations manager but it's not working out, so I'm back to doing everything myself again.'

Bryony had a superpower – when she walked into a room, it felt like the sun had just come out. She was kind and caring, she would do anything for anyone, and when you spoke with her, you felt you were the only person in the world. She was also highly principled, hard-working, full of ideas and a genius at wealth management. Clients immediately trusted her with their most personal hopes and fears, as well as their millions in life savings.

It didn't take long, when I interviewed her staff, to realise that Bryony's major problem was that she lacked some of the core Considered Architect skills that the business needed as it scaled. 'She won't ever give us any feedback,' said one person, 'so we have no idea how to improve.'

'She's so busy and spread so thin, that she becomes a bottleneck in the business,' said another.

'She wants everyone to be happy,' said a third. 'So we don't have tough conversations or say no to anything.'

Bryony had built a team of personal assistants, not a business. There was no strategy, no roadmap, no role descriptions, no milestones, processes or systems. I asked her what her approach to leading people was, and she replied, 'I love my team. I take them on inspiring off-sites twice a year where we share ideas and inspiration. I respect them enough to give them the freedom and autonomy they need to succeed.'

Bryony thought she gave people what they needed to thrive, but she didn't. She led people the way she would want to be led, over-indexing on inspiration and encouragement, not the way they needed to be led, with clarity, consistency and a plan.

The focus of our coaching was simple: craft clarity. People needed to understand what was expected of them, what the plan was, how they would know they were on or off track. Bryony introduced roadmapping sessions to her twice-yearly off-sites so that people not only felt inspired, but knew what they and their teammates would be focused on in the coming six months. She introduced clear role descriptions and targets for team members, and instituted monthly performance management meetings to track progress against the plan.

Many start-up founders buck against these processes, resenting the curbs on their freedom and the responsibility that comes from leading regular team meetings. Bryony, however, didn't mind any of that, so to start with, it was all plain sailing. The problems arose when it was time to have tough conversations.

'I hate upsetting people,' she said. 'So if people don't do a job well, I'd rather just do it myself than tell them.'

Bryony was a people-pleaser. She didn't want to upset clients, so she overpromised, then exhausted herself and her team trying to deliver. She didn't want to say no to key stakeholders, so she took on new projects or ideas that weren't in the plan she'd just crafted with her team. One member of her team was seriously underperforming and clearly not cut out for the job, but she avoided firing him.

Bryony could communicate to inspire but she couldn't Communicate to Manage (see Chapter 5), and she was driven by an ego need to please people, which made it challenging for her to have tough conversations (see

Chapter 7). As we honed those skills, and unpicked those needs, the workload became more manageable, and the team's performance improved. The process was incredibly challenging for Bryony as her default response of 'Say yes to everything and never upset anyone' was never far from the surface. It was only after a six-month performance review with a senior team member, that she had a true aha moment. 'I always thought I was being kind to people by avoiding tough conversations, but actually I was being selfish. I was putting my need to people-please above my team's need for feedback, clarity and a plan.'

Dial up or dial down your Considered Architect mode

Most founders I coach are natural Brave Warriors, so strengthening their Considered Architect mode is a major priority. This is the leadership mode you need most at the scale-up stage of business, but whatever stage of growth you're at, when you're delegating, managing individual or team performance, or building systems and processes, the Considered Architect mode is your friend.

If, on the other hand, you are a natural Considered Architect, there will be times when you need to dial that mode down. When you're at the start-up phase or need to pitch, innovate or act super-fast, you will need to dial it down so you can access your Brave Warrior mode. If you're at the grown-up stage of business, or need to inspire audiences or think strategically, you'll find it helpful to dial it down and lean into your Wise Monarch mode.

Dial up your Considered Architect when:	Dial down your Considered Architect when:
Delegating	You have strong functional leaders who need to be left to get on with their job
Developing and managing a high-performance team	Managing multiple stakeholder groups both inside and outside your organisation
Managing the performance of individual team members	Inspiring your audience
Designing and implementing systems and a plan	Focusing on long-term business strategy
Minimising confusion and managing risk	Spotting business risks and opportunities
You need to stay calm and considered	You need to energise others or act super-fast

What next?

Complete the Considered Architect self-test. Then ask yourself: 'Given the challenges I'm facing and our stage of business, do I need to dial up or dial down my Considered Architect mode?'

For most founders I coach, this is the mode of leadership they enjoy the least and avoid the most. If you know that's true for you, your future success depends on your ability to lean into this mode, even if it's just in a 'minimally viable' way. The Considered Architect Toolbox contains a set of exercises and ideas to help. These include an approach for establishing an annual cadence of business planning meetings, an exercise for helping you manage your focus, an approach to applying systems thinking, and exercises on how to delegate and think before you speak.

In the unlikely event that you are one of the rare founders who needs to dial down their Considered Architect mode:

▸ Focus on the Brave Warrior Toolbox if you need to act fast and sell hard.

▸ Read Chapter 4 (The Wise Monarch Mode) and Chapter 6 (Communicate to Influence) if you need to think strategically and inspire followership.

Considered Architect self-test	0 Very rarely	1 Rarely	2 Often	3 Very often
I am a systems thinker				
I am calm and unflappable				
I enjoy planning				
I solve problems at source				
I build high-performance teams				
I am good at managing people				
I am a good coach				
I like building processes				
I enjoy turning strategy into a roadmap				
I like creating order out of chaos				
My team know what's expected of them				
I am a team player				
I craft clarity				
I implement change in a considered way				
I manage and mitigate risk				
I think before I speak				
I drive accountability				

Considered Architect self-test	0 Very rarely	1 Rarely	2 Often	3 Very often
I am consistent				
I delegate, never abdicate				
I engage my team in key decision-making and planning				
People trust me and trust the plan we're working on				
I keep us focused on the plan and the next ninety days				
I prefer to do things properly even if it takes a bit more time				
I focus on attracting and retaining talent				
My attention is on the team and the plan				
Column totals: (Score 1 for rarely, 2 for often, 3 for very often)				
Add your column scores together to give you your **Considered Architect score:**				

Your Considered Architect score

If you scored 60–75: Congratulations, you are a Considered Architect. If you are at the scale-up stage of business, enjoy yourself. If you are at the start-up or grown-up stage, you may need to dial up your Brave Warrior or Wise Monarch modes. See the relevant sections of the Toolbox for how to do this.

If you scored 40–59: You can dial up your Considered Architect mode when needed. If you feel you need to dial it up more right now, look at the exercises in the Considered Architect Toolbox.

If you scored 0–39: You are very low on natural Considered Architect mode. Prioritise the exercises in the Considered Architect Toolbox, particularly if your business is in the scale-up phase.

4

The Wise Monarch Mode

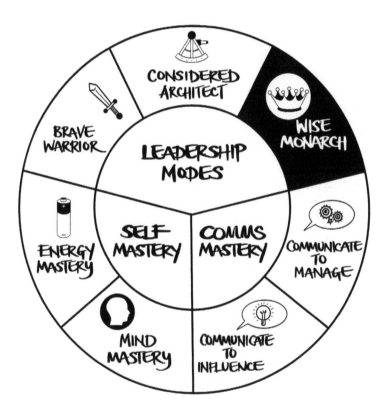

If we travelled back to a Viking clan or dropped into the AGM of a present-day multinational, we would immediately spot the monarch. The archetypal monarch is the true alpha of the group, exuding gravitas, authority and presence. They are inspirational leaders who understand the power of message and symbol.

Wise Monarchs recognise that hundreds, if not thousands, of people are looking to them for leadership, reassurance, confidence and belief. They communicate a vision of the future that people buy into, a mission that fills people with purpose, and a powerful strategy that provides direction and clarity.

You don't need the title of CEO to bring your Wise Monarch mode to a group. When I'm coaching a leadership team, I'm not the founder or the CEO, yet I'll pause before walking into the boardroom and put on my invisible crown. The team needs me to exude authority and calm confidence if we're going to have an effective working session. They do not need me showing up ruffled, stressed and out of control. It's my responsibility to park my fears and personal needs at the door, access my Wise Monarch mode and show up in service of the group.

As a monarch, you have both authority and power, and you need to wield them wisely in service of your organisation, or you'll come unstuck fast. The Wise Monarch doesn't lose touch with the operational nuts and bolts of their company, the changing culture and market in which they operate, or the mood and needs of their employees and stakeholders. The Wise Monarch doesn't believe their own hype.

The Wise Monarch in business

Wise Monarchs in business are inspiring figureheads and genius strategists. They are sure of themselves and their authority, and they exude personal presence. They take the 100,000-foot view of their business and focus on long-term strategic change. Wise Monarchs drive incredible value into large businesses and are essential to the success of organisations in the grown-up phase.

The Wise Monarch in business	
How to spot them	► Big-picture strategist ► Gravitas and presence ► Communicate for impact ► Politically astute ► Can appear arrogant
Most helpful for	► Providing direction and inspiration ► Thinking big picture and/or long term ► Reassuring or galvanising stakeholders ► Futureproofing the business ► Devising high-impact strategy
On a good day	A visionary corporate leader who instils confidence in their people and drives value into the business
On a bad day	An out-of-touch fantasist who believes their own hype
Stage of business	Grown-up

While the Brave Warrior charges at their adversary on the battlefield of business and the Considered Architect reviews battle plans at HQ, **the Wise Monarch decides how to win the war, builds alliances and inspires the troops and the folks back home.**

"

The Wise Monarch
is a master strategist
who oozes authority
and presence.

Your Wise Monarch
mode is crucial at
the grown-up stage,
but will falter if you
have a dysfunctional
leadership team or
lack operational grip.

The Wise Monarch provides people with a vision that excites and a sense of purpose that inspires and energises. They stay out of the operational weeds and focus on being a leader their people want to follow.

Wise Monarchs sense risks, threats, opportunities and change. Pro-surfers on the lookout for the perfect wave will sometimes trail their fingers in the sea. They know the sea so well that they can feel when the currents are changing and a wave is coming. Wise Monarchs trail their fingers in the commercial world they inhabit, picking up on shifts and changes that their business needs to adapt to.

The Wise Monarch is focused on big-picture strategic change that will elevate the business. 'Strategy' is a term often misused to refer to plans or goals, so let's get clear about how we're using the term here. At any time you have:

▸ A limited amount of resources available to you as a founder – whether that's time, money or people

▸ A series of business challenges and opportunities standing between you and your business objective

▸ A range of options for how you deploy your business's limited resources in pursuit of that objective

The strategic question is: 'How do we deploy these limited resources to create the biggest uplift and move us towards our objective?' Examples of brilliant strategies include Churchill's, 'If we win Paris, we win the war,' and Steve Jobs', 'If we own people's experience of music, we'll own their experience of computing' – my paraphrasing, not theirs.

The Wise Monarch has poise, gravitas and dignity. Indra Nooyi, the former CEO of Pepsi, says that the best advice she received on becoming CEO was to always walk with her head held high and a smile on her face when she arrived at headquarters in the morning. She knew that hundreds of employees would be watching as she walked across the plaza and that they would infer how well things were going by how relaxed and confident she looked.[5] **Wise Monarchs do not run around in a flap.**

Wise Monarchs know they need to combine self-confidence with humility. They will come unstuck if they buy into their own hype, if they use the power they have been given for selfish rather than collective ends, and if they fail to listen to the people around them – their stakeholders, their employees, their executives, their peers.

Wise Monarchs understand the responsibility that comes with power. We can each name as many deluded or despotic monarch leaders (Hitler, Nero) as we can principled or benevolent ones (Mandela, Marcus Aurelius). The Wise Monarch is one who understands the responsibility of the power they hold and uses that power, with humility, in service of the business.

The Wise Monarch in business has earned their authority. Their power is bestowed upon them by the people they lead and the stakeholders they serve. They know that power can be taken away at any moment if they lose their credibility or the confidence of their followers.

The Wise Monarch doesn't say or do anything that would be damaging if it appeared on the front cover of a newspaper. Words and deeds matter. They choose both wisely.

The Wise Monarch understands the political landscape they inhabit. They know that their business can fill with intrigue, machinations and gossip unless they actively manage and engage their stakeholders. Their executive team and board in particular are likely to be inhabited by highly intelligent and ambitious people who can become toxic, fast, if they are not rallying around a collective vision, strategy and way of working. Wise Monarchs are politically astute.

---

5 I Nooyi, 'On being one of the longest-serving female CEOs', *Fortune Magazine* (17 September 2019), www.youtube.com/watch?v=vRy-_w4cvT8, accessed 12 April 2022

Wise Monarchs are strong public speakers, and if they're not, they learn to be – fast. Think of the effort Steve Jobs put into his annual product launch presentations – months of practice just so he could nail one performance.[6] That makes sense when you recognise that millions of people were influenced by his presentation, and that the success of the business in the coming year would depend on his ability to capture the hearts and minds of his audience on that single occasion.

The Wise Monarch often has a powerful 'Be strong' driver. They have courage and are stoic in the face of difficulty. This also means that they can struggle to admit vulnerability and can become withdrawn under pressure.

The Wise Monarch mode and stages of business

The Wise Monarch mode in the grown-up stage

At the grown-up stage, the business should have the staff, infrastructure and finances that allow it to operate like a well-oiled machine. Operations are led by strong functional leaders who align through a regular cadence of strategic, planning and performance review meetings. Systems and processes are well-defined, effective and well-managed.

At this stage, the founder's challenge is to retain the organisation's entrepreneurial spirit and advantage, and prevent stagnation at all costs. They need to drive value into the organisation and avoid the ossification that can occur if the founder stays stuck in the operational weeds. If you keep architect-ing in a grown-up business, you will impede your team through micromanagement, miss the opportunities and threats in the marketplace and fail to provide the visionary leadership your business craves.

---

6   W Isaacson, *Steve Jobs: The exclusive biography* (Abacus, 2015)

In the grown-up stage, your business needs:

► A powerful business strategy, vision and mission

► An inspiring figurehead who stakeholders believe in

► A strong culture

It requires a founder who:

► Takes the 100,000-foot view of the business and the market

► Inspires large numbers of people

► Thinks strategically, not just operationally

► Understands and operates effectively within a highly political setting

The Wise Monarch mode is uniquely valuable at the grown-up stage of business. When drawing on your Wise Monarch mode:

► Your poise and gravitas reassure people.

► Your genius strategic thinking points the direction for your people to follow.

► Your ability to inspire an audience galvanises and reassures multiple stakeholder groups.

► Your unique combination of authority and humility protects the business from catastrophic, reputation-killing decisions and actions.

► Your focus on the changing currents in the business and the market ensures that you spot opportunities and threats – be they internal threats around culture, top team or strategy, or external threats around changing consumer needs or competition (among many others).

The Wise Monarch on a good day: a visionary corporate leader who instils confidence in their team and drives value into the business.

The Wise Monarch on a bad day: an out-of-touch fantasist who believes their own hype.

The vulnerabilities of the Wise Monarch mode

There are elements of the Wise Monarch leadership mode that can be helpful at every stage of business. Vision and strategy are powerful enablers of performance whether you are in the start-up, scale-up or grown-up phase. The ability to inspire an audience is helpful at any stage of the journey. But there are some vulnerabilities inherent in leading purely from your Wise Monarch mode.

Wise Monarch leadership works when you have a high-performing executive team that has a strong operational grip on the business. This high-performing team needs to be aligned around a vision, strategy and plan; to work effectively and respectfully with each other; and to drive collaboration between their departments. Where alignment or operational grip is lacking, where there are siloes in the business or an unhealthy culture, it is not enough to point to the strategic direction and hope. You need to manage your top team. You need to keep an eye on culture. You need to drive, not just set, strategy. These are moments where you need to access your Considered Architect mode to lead with a firmer operational grip.

The Wise Monarch is uniquely susceptible to believing their own hype. There are few people around them brave enough to speak truth to power. The Wise Monarch who doesn't seek and encourage feedback can quickly find themselves ousted when their stakeholders lose confidence in their leadership.

CASE STUDY: PHIL

Most founders I work with are Brave Warriors who need to access more Considered Architect energy. Phil was the exception. Phil had worked for twenty years as an operational leader in a large organisation before launching his own business, and he was a natural Considered Architect.

Phil launched his business with significant backing from a number of corporate investors and, for the first four years, things were good as he went about doing the things he did best. He hired and managed top talent, built a high-performance team, managed investors and clients, and set up systems and processes. Phil's natural reserve and thoughtfulness, along with his incredibly strong operational grip, were an enormous benefit to the company at the scale-up stage.

By the time the Covid-19 pandemic hit, Phil had a global team of over eighty people and a top team who managed most day-to-day operations. He called me following the results of his annual employee engagement survey. 'The scores are generally good,' he said. 'But there are a couple of things that concern me – in particular, our scores for "I am inspired by the company and I'm proud to work here", which aren't what I'd like them to be.'

Phil and I talked about leadership modes and he clearly identified himself as a Considered Architect. 'There are certain elements of the Wise Monarch mode that I think I do well,' he said. 'I'm pretty good at stakeholder management and all our investors are happy. I'm very connected to our industry and sector and I'm good at spotting trends and opportunities that may affect the business, but I don't like the whole public speaking thing and really dislike being the centre of attention. And I'm not sure how strategic my thinking is. We always have a plan and clearly stated goals, but I suspect I'm a bit too much in the weeds to be genuinely strategic.'

We explored what the business needed from Phil as it entered the grown-up phase, and he saw that he needed to pull away from day-to-day operations. He needed to focus his attention on the 100,000-foot strategic view, while providing the visible and inspirational leadership his people were asking for.

We ran a strategic off-site with his top team and posed the question, 'What business strengths do we have that we could double down on to put clear blue water between us and the competition?' The team identified three compelling strategic pillars around which to orient their efforts and immediately got to work tweaking their plans and operations accordingly. Phil returned from the off-site galvanised and energised. He hired an acting coach to help with his public speaking and a PR consultant to get him onto the right stages to share his message. A couple of weeks ago, I watched as Phil metaphorically banged the desk while being interviewed on CNN.

Bang! Hello, inspirational Wise Monarch.

Dial up or dial down your Wise Monarch mode

The Wise Monarch mode most closely correlates with pure leadership as described in most business books, and it is the style you will depend upon as your business reaches the grown-up stage. But there are times during the start-up and the scale-up phases where your team, employees and stakeholders need you to draw from this leadership mode. When your business needs you to be the inspirational figurehead, when you need to focus on strategy or complex political situations, the Wise Monarch mode is your friend.

You may be reading this chapter thinking, 'Yes, I want to be a Wise Monarch!' Most of my clients do. The gravitas and authority, the vision and the strategy of the Wise Monarch are appealing to many founders. The bad news is that there are plenty of times, whatever stage of business you're at, where you'll need to dial down this mode. If you have a weak leadership team and need strong operational grip, if you have poor processes and systems, if you need to manage projects or performance, or to roll up your sleeves and drive short-term urgent change, you'll need to dial it down and access one of the other leadership modes.

Dial up your Wise Monarch when:	Dial down your Wise Monarch when:
Inspiring with gravitas and presence	Strong operational grip is required
Being a figurehead	Taking personal action and rolling your sleeves up
Strategising and futureproofing	Driving short-term, urgent change
Managing complex internal or external politics	Managing projects or performance
Focusing on purpose, vision, brand, culture or organisational health	Focusing on systems, processes or operations

What next?

Complete the Wise Monarch self-test. Then ask yourself: 'Given the challenges I'm facing and our stage of business, do I need to dial up or dial down my Wise Monarch?'

If your business needs you to dial up your Wise Monarch mode you'll find exercises in the Toolbox to help you think strategically, politically and culturally, as well as an approach to building a personal leadership brand while staying humble and in service of your business.

If, on the other hand, you need to dial down your Wise Monarch, take personal action and drive urgent, short-term change, focus on the exercises in the Brave Warrior Toolbox. Alternatively, if your business lacks strong operational grip, or your leadership team is dysfunctional or siloed, focus on the Considered Architect Toolbox to help you manage people, performance and systems.

Wise Monarch self-test	0 Very rarely	1 Rarely	2 Often	3 Very often
I have a compelling vision that inspires people				
I focus on the big picture				
I am a strategic thinker				
I have gravitas and presence				
I am politically astute				
I am good at rallying the troops				
I am excellent at stakeholder management				
My communication is high impact				
I am good at reassuring and influencing stakeholders				
I focus on driving long-term value into the business				
I think about futureproofing the business				
I am good at spotting threats and opportunities				
I drive strategic change				
I don't say anything that would be damaging if it was on the front cover of a newspaper				

Wise Monarch self-test	0 Very rarely	1 Rarely	2 Often	3 Very often
I focus on the responsibilities, not the rights of leadership				
I invite feedback and challenge				
I act in service of the business, not in service of myself				
I am an inspiring public speaker				
I focus on long-term strategy				
I do powerful, rather than just quick/easy things				
I focus on culture				
I often talk about purpose, strategy and values				
I keep abreast of trends, competition and change				
I am a leader who people want to follow				
I have strong external networks				
Column totals: (Score 1 for rarely, 2 for often, 3 for very often)				
Add your column scores together to give you your **Wise Monarch score:**				

Your Wise Monarch score

If you scored 60–75: Congratulations, you are a Wise Monarch. If you are at the grown-up stage of business – with a strong executive team managing business operations – enjoy yourself.

If you are at the start-up or grown-up stage, or if your team is underperforming, you may need to lean into your Brave Warrior or Considered Architect modes. See the relevant sections of the Toolbox for how to do this.

If you scored 40–59: You can dial up your Wise Monarch mode when needed. If you feel you need to dial it up more right now, look at the exercises in the Wise Monarch Toolbox.

If you scored 0–39: You are very low on natural Wise Monarch mode. Prioritise the exercises in the Wise Monarch Toolbox, particularly if your business is at the grown-up phase.

Part One Summary: The Three Leadership Modes And How To Flex Them

The Brave Warrior is single-minded, focused and driven in pursuit of a win. The Brave Warrior mode is brilliantly suited to the start-up phase of business. At the scale-up stage, the Brave Warrior mode is often destructive and counterproductive.

The Considered Architect is a calm planner, thoughtful designer and genius systems thinker. The Considered Architect mode is worth its weight in gold at the scale-up stage. As a business reaches the grown-up stage, the Considered Architect can fail to provide the visionary or strategic leadership the business needs to thrive.

The Wise Monarch is the alpha of the group, exuding gravitas, authority and presence. The Wise Monarch mode is crucial at the grown-up stage of business. The Wise Monarch will struggle if they have a dysfunctional leadership team, lack operational grip or start to believe their own hype.

How well suited is your preferred mode to the stage of business you're at and/or the challenges you're currently facing? Do you need to flex and lean into another leadership mode at this stage?

At its core, your ability to flex your leadership comes down to two key things:

- ▸ Your ability to dial each leadership mode up or down
- ▸ Your awareness of when to do that

If you have completed the self-tests, you may already have a good sense of which leadership mode you need to strengthen most. If you'd like to, you can jump straight to the Toolbox at the back of the book and dive in to the relevant section. But if you're not quite ready for that, here's a simple two-step process that you can start applying immediately.

Step 1: Anchor your Warrior, Architect and Monarch role models

First, you need to anchor the three different leadership modes into your subconscious so you can easily dial them up or down as the situation requires. Each leadership mode has a distinct energy, focus, objective and impact, and one of the easiest ways to anchor these in your mind is to think of an exemplar of each mode. Think of someone you know and admire, a model of that style of leadership whom you can hold in your mind as a reminder of that way of being whenever you need to access it.

Start with a Brave Warrior. In my mind, Matthias is one of my most warrior-like clients. He rarely smiles, he walks with drive and purpose, and he doesn't do small talk. He emanates single-minded focus and is a down-to-business guy. Matthias powers through discussion points with speed, determination and focus. He has his eye on the goal at all times. He talks tactics, solutions, problem-solving, and he's fast, efficient, lean. He knows what he thinks and says it, normally first in a team meeting. Matthias is the person I would want to lead me if we were in a crisis.

The Considered Architect is trickier to spot, simply because they're often quieter, more thoughtful and likely to speak least and last. Joseph is one of my most architect-like clients. He's calm and quite subdued; he thinks before he speaks and is often last to voice an opinion in a meeting. He's introverted and his energy seems to flow inwards rather than filling up and overwhelming the room. He's also one of the most reliable people I know: he always does what he says he's going to do. His emails are thoughtful, well put-together and typo-free. Joseph would never have a meeting without an agenda that's been circulated ahead of time. At the end of each meeting, he ensures everyone is clear on what's been agreed and he follows up, always, with meeting notes. Joseph is the person I would want to lead me if we needed to create order out of chaos.

The Wise Monarch exudes gravitas and their authority fills the room like a gravitational pull. Miriam is one of my most monarch-like clients. She is always immaculately dressed and unflappable, holds her head high and has the poise and gravitas of a member of the royal family. Miriam speaks calmly and her comments are strategic and inspiring. She expects to be treated with respect, and she is. She is magnanimous, gracious and undeniably powerful. She doesn't suffer fools or mistakes and she expects the best from everyone – and most of the time, her people deliver just that. Miriam is the person I would want to lead me if we needed to think big picture.

Who are your Matthias, Joseph and Miriam? Think of the three people who best embody these three leadership modes and keep them in mind. Next time you need to lean into a leadership mode that is not your strongest, remind yourself to 'Do a Joseph' or 'Do a Miriam'.

Step 2: Understand when to dial each mode up or down

Build a habit of self-reflection. Ask yourself on a regular basis, 'What does this project/team/day/month/quarter/encounter/ stage require of me as a founder?' If you don't, you'll find that you have slipped back into your default leadership mode more days than not.

Like any habit, you need to repeatedly engage in this process of self-reflection until it becomes second nature. Start right now. Think of a challenge you are currently facing in the business. Which mode of leadership is best suited to solving that challenge? Now think of an important meeting you have coming up, and what you want to achieve in it. Which mode of leadership will enable you to achieve that?

If you are ready and willing to embed this new habit of self-reflection, make a commitment to yourself to reflect like this every day. As you write your to-do list for the day, answer these questions:

▸ Which mode of leadership do I need to lean into today?

▸ How can I show up to best enable my team and my business to achieve success today?

Two crucial caveats

1. It is likely that there are specific leadership skills you will need to learn to be effective in each mode – particularly around different communication styles. You won't be an effective Considered Architect unless you learn to Communicate to Manage, and you can't be an effective Wise Monarch unless you know how to Communicate to Influence. We'll look at this more in Part Two.

2. You can't manage your leadership mode unless you are able to manage yourself. If you are full of resentment, raging ego needs or negative beliefs, you're not going to be able to adapt your leadership mode effectively. Similarly if you are exhausted, hungover or hopped up on caffeine, you won't do a great job of dialling up and down your different leadership modes.

In Part Two we look at two crucial styles of communication and in Part Three we look at managing yourself. Think of these three elements – leadership modes, communication styles and self-management – as the three legs of your founder survival stool. You need all three legs for the stool to be firm. If you're trying to operate just on leadership modes, without strengthening communications and self-management, it's like sitting on a one-legged stool – unstable, hard work and likely to break.

Questions to ask yourself

▶ Which is your preferred leadership mode – Brave Warrior, Considered Architect or Wise Monarch?

▶ How well suited is your preferred mode to the stage of business you're at and/or the challenges you're currently facing?

▶ Which leadership mode do you most need to dial up and which do you need to dial down?

The Toolbox

In the Toolbox at the end of this book you will find a series of exercises that will help you dial up each of these different leadership modes:

Brave Warrior tools

1. Dial up vision
2. Dial up self-belief
3. Get the adrenaline pumping
4. Hang out with other warriors
5. Create a personal pledge

Considered Architect tools

1. Introduce an annual cadence of business planning meetings
2. Delegate, don't abdicate
3. Think systemically
4. Think before you speak
5. Manage your focus

The ability to flex your leadership mode to the needs of your business is the cornerstone of founder survival.

Wise Monarch tools

1. Strengthen your strategic-thinking muscle
2. Think politically
3. Think culturally
4. Look up and out and build your personal board
5. Stay humble and in service of the business

PART TWO

COMMS MASTERY

An Introduction To Comms Mastery

Marie was an extraordinary marketeer. After twelve years in a large business-to-business multinational, Marie spotted an opportunity in the content creation space, providing media services to an underserved but exploding sector. She created a powerful product offering, convinced an existing contact to become an early adopter of her new company's services and launched her own company.

Marie hired me two years later. By that stage, she had secured significant capital investment and the business was operating in three territories with sixty staff. She called me, stressed and overwhelmed, when her second COO in two years quit.

'I just can't trust anyone in that role,' she said. 'I hire smart people, I give them freedom and autonomy, and they screw everything up. People hate them, everyone comes to me for answers, then the COO gets upset when I give them. I hired a COO because I hate managing people and systems, but we've ended up with worse systems and unhappier people than we had on day one. I don't know what the solution is.'

I suggested we gathered 360-degree feedback to get her team's perspective on what was happening. The results were brutal. 'We don't see Marie for weeks on end because she's on the road meeting clients and running projects, then she comes into the office and blows up everything we've been working on,' said one person.

'Marie is the worst manager I have ever worked with,' said another. 'She changes her mind constantly, we don't know where we stand, sometimes we are stuck waiting for weeks for a decision and we can't get hold of her, other times she's in the minutiae of every decision we make and nothing we do is right.'

Everyone admired her strategic brain and loved her when she was communicating to inspire people. On stage, on TV, at a client pitch, Marie was one of the most brilliant communicators they'd met. When it came to communicating to manage people, however, Marie just simply couldn't or wouldn't do it.

When she hired a COO, she absented herself from the office so she could spend time with strategic partners. When she got calls from staff members complaining about things, she barked at the COO. When she saw work output she didn't like, she barked at the COO. Every time she was pulled into something operational, she was full of resentment and barked at the COO.

The problem here wasn't that the COO was a bad fit, it was that Marie couldn't Communicate to Manage. She didn't delegate – she abdicated. She operated on a 'hire and hope' approach to performance management. She flipped between being a completely absent CEO, then, when she did check in with the business, she micromanaged and reversed decisions that had been made in her absence. She didn't set her COO up for success, didn't manage them or their work, didn't respond effectively to problems and challenges they had and, as a result, she completely disempowered them and their work. This sent mixed messages to her team and destabilised the entire business.

Marie is not uncommon among the founders who hire me. The number-one issue most clients say they are struggling with is their people. They ask:

▸ Why aren't my staff performing?

▸ Why are my team complaining?

▸ Why are my investors/partners/co-founders such a pain?

Much of the time, these problems turn out to be symptoms of poor leadership communication.

Let's be clear. Becoming a good communicator will not immediately turn every person into a super employee, happy customer or easy investor. Sometimes employees are a poor fit and need to be exited. Sometimes a customer will leave no matter what you do, and you will need to minimise the damage. Sometimes investors or other stakeholders will be obstreperous for the sake of it, and you will need to dig deep into reserves of patience to manage them.

Nevertheless, a founder's communication style often contributes to or exacerbates the people problems they so often complain about as their business starts to grow. Part Two of this book gives you the tools you need to prevent that.

The two styles of communication

To survive and thrive as a founder, you need to master two very different sets of communication skills. You need to be able to:

1. Communicate to Manage
2. Communicate to Influence

Communicating to Manage involves the ability to:

▸ Delegate effectively

▸ Give feedback and have tough conversations gracefully

▸ Coach your people

▸ Elicit high performance from your leadership team

Communicating to Influence involves the ability to:

▸ Sell effectively

▸ Present with gravitas

▸ Speak in public

▸ Communicate your leadership brand

▸ Manage stakeholders, including investors

> **The number-one problem clients approach me with is 'people'.**
>
> **Most of the time, these problems are symptoms of poor leadership communication.**

Most founders have mastered some, but not all, of these skills. If they are a Brave Warrior, they're normally good at selling. If they are a Considered Architect, they're normally skilled at managing, and if they are a Wise Monarch, they may excel at influencing stakeholders and communicating their brand. Rarely, though, do founders nail all the communication skills they're going to need as their business scales.

Just as each business stage requires a different mode of leadership, so too does it call upon different communication styles. While it's helpful to master both styles regardless of your stage of business growth, you'll also find it helpful to know when you are most likely to need to over-index on each.

At the start-up stage, you need to be able to Communicate to Influence as you present and pitch your idea.

At the scale-up stage, you need to be able to Communicate to Manage, as your growing company needs you to delegate tasks, coach your team and develop a high-performing team.

At the grown-up stage, you need to lean on your Communicate to Influence style once more as you manage stakeholders and represent your brand.

In the next two chapters, we'll explore the basics of communicating to manage and communicating to influence. At the end of the book, you'll find a helpful Toolbox to help you apply those basics to a variety of typical founder challenges.

Comms Mastery at the start-up, scale-up and grown-up stage			
	At the start-up stage, you need to be able to:	**At the scale-up stage, you also need to be able to:**	**At the grown-up stage, you also need to be able to:**
Communicate to Influence	Sell/ Influence one-to-one Present well Pitch		Communicate brand Speak well publicly Influence one to many Manage stakeholders
Communicate to Manage		Delegate effectively Give feedback Have tough conversations gracefully Coach your people Elicit high performance from your team	

5

Communicate To Manage

What do you say when your direct reports are underperforming? What do you do when your leadership team is floundering? What's your approach to managing people?

If you said, 'I hire great people then let them get on with it,' that's great in principle. In reality, though, this often ends up as the 'hire and hope' approach, or the 'abdicate responsibility, dislike what you see, micromanage then fire' approach.

If you said, 'I trust that people are adults and I give them the freedom and autonomy I would want,' again, that's great in principle. In reality, though, if your employees needed what you need they'd be a founder, not an employee.

If you said, 'Honestly, I just get really pissed off, stay up at night stewing about it, clumsily try to say something, more often than not lose patience or my temper, and eventually fire them,' thanks for being honest. This section is for you!

For most Brave Warrior or Wise Monarch founders, communicating to manage is one of the skills they lack the most, and one of the activities they enjoy the least. If you are a Warrior or a Monarch, play to your strengths and delegate as much management responsibility as possible to a COO, your leadership team and/or your EA. Even as you do this, though, you still need to understand how to manage those people. This chapter gives you the tools to do that. Think of this as the 'minimally viable management' chapter.

The Communicate to Manage style

At its core, the Communicate to Manage style is about giving your people what they need from you to be successful in their roles, in a way that works for them. *You* may not need clarity, feedback, rules or consistency, but your team does, and your job is to set them up for success.

"

For most Brave Warrior or Wise Monarch founders, communicating to manage is one of the skills they lack the most and enjoy the least, so think of this as the 'minimally viable management' chapter.

Communicating to manage is about focusing your attention on what you want to happen, and communicating in a way that enables that. It's about focusing on constructive solutions and the future, not who did what to whom, when and why. It's about solutions, not blame.

The Communicate to Manage style is about your ability to manage your emotions, and have tough conversations gracefully and honestly, with the best interests of your business and team at heart. It is a service and a responsibility. It's putting your needs and wants (to be right, to be flexible, to be autonomous) on the back burner, so you can enable success from the people who make your vision come true.

When faced with any problem, including 'people problems', you have three rational options:

1. Accept the problem fully, with a peaceful heart, knowing that you, and the business, can live with it.

2. Walk away from the problem. Let the employee or client go; buy out the partner or investor.

3. Do something to change the problem – and the only thing you can change is what you think, do or say.

These are the rational options.

What most of us do, though, is pick an irrational and unhelpful option 4: do nothing, whinge to our friends, nurse our resentments and wait for the other person to miraculously change. Option 4 doesn't do you or the business any good at all. It may soothe your ego, but it doesn't solve the problems you face.

If you decide that you or the business can't take the first option to accept the problem – because, for example, the underperformance is too great – nor are you ready to take the second and walk away – perhaps because the relationship is too important – you are left with option 3: change what you think, do or say.

To take this option, there are some core principles of the Communicate to Manage style that you need to know:

- Contract 4R clarity
- The Manage Mindset Formula
- The Karpman Drama Triangle

Once you understand these, you'll be able to diagnose where you may be stumbling, and what to do about it.

Core principles of the Communicate to Manage style

1. Contract 4R clarity

One of the biggest differences between the people who found businesses and the people who work for them is the degree of uncertainty they are comfortable with. If you are reading this book, it's likely that you are comfortable with a high degree of uncertainty – if you weren't, you wouldn't be a founder. Founders typically need autonomy and freedom more than they need certainty and clarity.

Your people, on the other hand, have chosen to take the salary rather than the risk. They are likely to need much more certainty and clarity than you do, and it's your job to provide it. Your responsibility as a founder is to ensure, rather than assume, that the team you manage and the people you lead have enough clarity to be able to perform well. It's a trite but helpful truism that 'When you assume, you make an ass out of u and me.' (Sorry!) When you assume people know what's expected, or that they will behave in certain ways, or that they will just work it all out, you set them up to fail and set yourself up for frustration, resentment and workdays filled with 'people problems'.

The solution I recommend to founders is that they 'contract 4R clarity' with their direct reports or team. This is a simple yet powerful concept that helps founders remember the four things individuals and teams need to know to be high-performing.

In coaching, the term 'contracting' refers to the process of agreeing at the start of a relationship what the mutual expectations are. The 4Rs are the things you need to agree when you start work with a new team or team member. They are:

1. Roles/responsibilities

2. Rules

3. Results/roadmap

4. Review

Let's look at each of these in turn.

Roles/responsibilities

People need to understand what their role is. They need clarity about what they're responsible for and what decision-making power they have. They also need you to clarify the swim lanes between their and others' roles. A dusty job description in a forgotten folder won't cut it.

Rules

One major cause of friction with your direct reports and between team members will be a lack of clarity around what you need and expect of one another behaviourally. Craft a set of operating principles, ideally with your team. Refer to them regularly in your meetings, one-to-ones and performance reviews.

Results/roadmap

People need to be clear on the results you expect from them, and when. They also need to know one another's timelines,

Communicating to
manage is about
giving people
what they need to
be successful in
their roles.

deliverables and goals. There are a number of approaches to setting individual and team goals and plans. You can use key performance indicators (KPIs) or objectives and key results (OKRs). You can use a critical path analysis, a Gantt chart or any number of project management software packages. (For more on strategic planning and OKRs, see the Toolbox at the back of the book.)

Whichever approach you use, your people need to be clear on what the goals are for at least the next ninety days and which of those results they are personally responsible for.

Review

People need accountability. They need to know when you will review performance, update plans and refine agreements together. Aim to have review sessions with your direct reports individually, and with the team as a whole, at least once a quarter. Once you've agreed and set dates for these meetings, don't cancel them, unless you want your people to think their performance is unimportant.

You can contract 4R clarity with your team by creating a team charter – a framework for this is included in the Toolbox.

2. The Manage Mindset Formula

While the 4Rs tells you *what* you need to communicate about, the Manage Mindset Formula helps you remember the mindset you need to employ to do that effectively, and to overcome one of the biggest blockers to successful people management, namely, the desire to avoid 'difficult conversations'.

Most of us avoid conversations we assume will be difficult because we don't like conflict or upsetting people. In reality, we cause more damage by avoiding these discussions or by having them poorly.

When you prepare for any management conversation that feels difficult, keep in mind the Manage Mindset Formula:

The Manage Mindset = Brave + Kind + Clean

Brave

Your team needs honest, constructive feedback from you about what they are doing well and what they could do better. You need to put their need for constructive feedback ahead of your own discomfort about having these conversations. Be brave.

Kind

If the only time you ever give feedback is when things are going wrong and you're frustrated, you won't help your direct reports improve. Genuine praise and signs of appreciation are as powerful in shaping behaviour as constructive criticism. Be kind.

Clean

Use 'clean' rather than 'charged' language when communicating to manage. Charged language is highly emotive and will likely trigger a defensive reaction. Clean language removes as much judgement, accusation and emotion from the conversation as possible and allows for open and constructive dialogue. Keep it clean.

See the Toolbox for how to use the Manage Mindset to deliver effective feedback.

3. The Karpman Drama Triangle

No Communicate to Manage discussion would be complete without mention of the brilliant Karpman Drama Triangle.[7] Stephen Karpman is a psychiatrist of the Transactional Analysis tradition who studied the psychology of interpersonal relationships. He created the Karpman Drama Triangle to illustrate the subconscious games at play in people's relationships with others.

---

7   S Karpman, 'Fairy tales and script drama analysis', *Transactional Analysis Bulletin*, 7/26 (1968), 39–43

Karpman proposed that, through formative experience, we learn to gain power in any relationship by adopting one of three standard 'positions':

1. **Persecutor** – 'I'm right, you're wrong. I'm powerful. I'm not responsible. You're to blame.'

2. **Victim** – 'I'm always wrong. I'm powerless. I'm not responsible. Everyone is nasty to me and it's not fair.'

3. **Rescuer** – 'I'll fix it. I'm powerful, in a helpful elf, "please love me" kind of way. Don't worry, I'll take responsibility for everything.'

Each of us tends to move to one of these three positions when under pressure, but here's the problem: when you find yourself in one of these three mindset positions, you simply perpetuate your own, and everyone else's, position:

▸ If you rescue, victims cannot rescue themselves and stay victims, persecutors cannot make amends and stay persecutors.

▸ If you persecute, victims' put-upon status is reinforced, rescuers try harder until they snap.

▸ If you play the victim people continue either to persecute you or to rescue you.

Things get really hairy when people move around the triangle together. Let's imagine you're managing someone who regularly shows up as the 'victim'. Let's call this person Whinging Wally.

Whenever you talk with Whinging Wally, he's complaining. He's whining about the finance department, or the clients, the ops team or the lawyers. He's sorry he missed the deadline, he really did try, he's been so busy, so overwhelmed, it's not his fault.

Being a kind and caring manager, you want to help Whinging Wally, so you adopt a can-do attitude and say things like, 'Have you thought about this?' or, 'Don't get stressed – we can work it out. Here, let me do that for you.' You help. You lean in. You jump into the triangle and rescue him.

What you've failed to understand is that Whinging Wally quite enjoys whinging. There's a payoff to being helpless. No one expects much of him and everyone tries to rescue him. So Whinging Wally keeps whining and complaining. He doesn't do anything to help himself, and you get more and more frustrated.

One day, you snap. You've had just about enough of the constant complaints and whining, and bark, 'Oh for God's sake, Wally, enough with the complaining.' Now you've moved around the triangle and you've become the persecutor.

Whinging Wally looks at you like he's been slapped. Then in full victim mode, he says, 'You see! Everyone's always horrible to me.'

Now imagine you're managing someone who plays the persecutor role. Let's call them Angry Angie.

You avoid tricky conversations with Angry Angie because you don't want to rouse her ire. When you see Angry Angie roll her eyes in meetings, you ignore it. You work around her rudeness and bad moods. You say things like, 'Let me take that, Angie's got a lot on today,' or, 'I won't mention this today because Angie's in a bad mood.' You don't share feedback, you bite your tongue, and you accept every slammed phone and aggressive comment Angry Angie makes.

Without realising it, you're enabling Angry Angie, and you're in the triangle rescuing her. Gradually though, your resentment starts to build and one day you find yourself whinging and complaining about Angie. You've become the victim. Or you get so frustrated that you snap, lose your temper and become the persecutor yourself.

Luckily, you can escape the triangle by developing a fourth position, one that sits outside the triangle. Let's call this the leveller/observer position, the basic premise of which is:

► 'I'm OK, you're OK, and we have a challenge between us we need to fix.'

- ‣ 'I'm responsible for my words, thoughts, deeds. You're responsible for yours.'
- ‣ 'I notice the drama. I'm happy to discuss it, and I'm not getting into it.'

When you're in the leveller/observer role, you have very different conversations with Whinging Wally or Angry Angie. You address issues as they arise in a brave, clean and kind way. You have conversations that sound something like this:

'Wally, I notice that in our one-to-ones, you're often focused on what's not working or why you can't do something, and that's having a negative impact. Moving forward, my request is that you come to our meetings with suggestions for solutions to the problems you're facing, or specific requests for support that you need from me.'

'Angie, I noticed that you rolled your eyes in today's meeting and that concerns me. From now on, please remain aware of the impact of your behaviour on others. If you disagree with something I'm saying, speak up, or if you are frustrated or angry, talk to me one-to-one.'

Staying in the triangle doesn't help you or anyone else and the sooner you get out of it, the sooner the others will too.

CASE STUDY: OLIVIA

Olivia was the founder of a successful VC-backed alcohol-free drinks company in the USA. Her company was four years old and was experiencing astronomical year-on-year growth. She had just hired her first three VPs when she started coaching with me.

'I hired VPs because I was managing way too many junior people,' she told me. 'But right now, my VPs are causing more problems than anything else. They don't get on with one another, or the team, and everyone is coming to me to complain all the time.'

I asked her about her management communication style and she said, 'I'm not sure I have one. For the first two years, we were bootstrapping everything so we just got on with it together. Maybe I've hired VPs who are a wrong cultural fit.'

During my interviews with Olivia's key people, it became obvious that there were some structural problems at play:

- The broader team didn't like the fact that they were now being managed by newcomers to the business. When they didn't like what the new VPs said, they worked around them and went directly to Olivia. Olivia's response was to either solve their problems or listen to their tales of woe.

- The VPs were unclear on the boundaries of their responsibilities, the results they were driving for, or the roadmap the company was taking to achieve its vision. They were jostling for clarity, arguing about who had decision-making authority and who should be consulted on everything, from marketing to sales to operations.

- No one really knew what was expected of them culturally or behaviourally. As Olivia became more distant structurally, her influence waned and all sorts of behaviour-related personal resentments had bubbled up in the broader team.

I introduced Olivia to the Karpman Drama Triangle and asked her if she thought her tendency was to shift into the victim, persecutor or rescuer role in her relationships with others.

'I probably start as the rescuer,' she said. 'I want people to be happy and I don't like conflict, so my initial reaction is to fix people's problems or be a kind ear. If that doesn't work, I'll get frustrated and angry and move towards the persecutor or victim in my mind. But because I dislike confrontation, I'm unlikely to explode, and more likely just to withdraw and ignore the problem.'

We looked at the Manage Mindset Formula and how to deliver feedback to people in a kind, brave and clean way. Olivia's tendency was to avoid 'brave' conversations and hope problems solved themselves. The lightbulb moment came when she realised that having honest and brave conversations before issues became a massive problem was actually kinder than letting problems fester and grow. She started to use a simple feedback process to communicate about problems as soon as they appeared. (For more, see the Toolbox at the back of the book.)

With these pieces in place, we looked at other structural problems. We set up a leadership off-site where she and the VPs clarified their roles and responsibilities and their operational roadmap. Then she and her newly hired head of people ran a brilliant full-team off-site where everyone explored what they wanted the company 'rules' to be, ie the behavioural values or operating principles.

While this solved the vast majority of problems Olivia had been experiencing, it also made clear that one of her two VP hires was a poor cultural fit, so Olivia respectfully and firmly fired her.

'That was a really important moment for the whole company,' her head of people told me afterwards. 'People saw that Olivia was serious about the rules and roadmap, and that people who didn't get on board would be asked to leave. What you permit, you promote as a leader,' she went on to say. 'And now that Olivia doesn't permit unhelpful behaviour or poor performance, the whole company is stepping up.'

Olivia now has a team of VPs who effectively and collectively run the day-to-day operation of the business, which has freed up time for her to secure a significant round of funding.

What next?

Complete the Communicate to Manage self-test. Then ask yourself: 'Given the challenges I'm facing and our stage of business, do I need to strengthen my Communicate to Manage skills?'

If you do, focus on the exercises in the Communicate to Manage Toolbox. The Toolbox contains two exercises to help you Communicate to Manage individuals: a simple three-step process for delivering effective feedback and five questions you can use to coach for performance. The Toolbox also contains three exercises to help you Communicate to Manage with your team, including an approach to use to create a team charter, a guide for how to run a team process review and guidance for managing team dynamics.

Communicate to Manage self-test	0 Very rarely	1 Rarely	2 Often	3 Very often
I delegate effectively				
I give good feedback				
I am good at having tough conversations				
I know how to get the best from people				
I elicit high performance from my team				
I know how to manage conflict in a group				
I understand and manage group dynamics				
I ensure dysfunction in my team is resolved				
I encourage healthy debate				
I ensure disagreements are surfaced and resolved				
My team members are clear on their roles/responsibilities				
People know the results they are responsible for				
My team know what our operating principles or behavioural values are				
I hold people accountable for upholding behavioural values				
I foster effective collaboration in my team				
If I have a problem with someone, I talk to them about it				
I regularly review people's performance with them				

Communicate to Manage self-test	0 Very rarely	1 Rarely	2 Often	3 Very often
My team and I regularly review our plan and results				
I communicate in a brave, kind and clean way				
I talk to people, not about them				
I avoid rescuing people				
I avoid people-pleasing				
I manage my emotions; I don't manage from them				
I focus on solutions not problems				
I lead effective meetings				
Column totals: (Score 1 for rarely, 2 for often, 3 for very often)				
Add your column scores together to give you your **Communicate to Manage score:**				

Your Communicate to Manage score

If you scored 60–75: Congratulations, you have mastered the Communicate to Manage style. Feel free to jump to the next section.

If you scored 40–59: You have mastered some of the key Communicate to Manage skills. Look at the Communicate to Manage Tools in the Toolbox to see which skills you may need to strengthen.

If you scored 0–39: You need to strengthen your Communicate to Manage skills. Prioritise the exercises in the Communicate to Manage Tools in the Toolbox.

6

Communicate To Influence

What's the first thing you think of when preparing for an important meeting or presentation?

If it's 'The point I need to make...' or 'The information I need to impart...', then you're not influencing as well as you think you are.

If it's 'The impact I want to create...' or 'The purpose of the meeting/presentation...', you are doing a better job of influencing your audience.

If it's 'What my audience needs from me, what I need from them and how to craft my communication to enable both those things to happen...' then you're an influencing ninja. Feel free to skip this chapter.

Your ability to survive and thrive as a founder is dependent on your ability to influence others, whether that's one-to-one in pitches, one to a group in presentations, or one to many on a stage. As your business grows and you shift from Brave Warrior to Wise Monarch, you'll also need to influence politics, culture and stakeholders, as well as manage your own leadership brand through thoughtful communication.

As a founder, it's likely that you already know a fair amount about influence and have nailed one or two key influencing skills, such as pitching and presenting. But it's equally likely that there are some areas where your influencing skills may be letting you down. The purpose of this chapter is to plug those gaps.

The Communicate to Influence style

At its core, communicating to influence is about understanding how people form impressions and make decisions, then adapting your communication in line with that. While communicating to manage is about giving your people what they need to be successful in their roles, communicating to influence

Communicating to influence is about being a leader people want to follow.

is about being someone people want to follow. Communicating to manage is fine when you have direct management responsibility, but you need to Communicate to Influence when you want people who don't work directly for you to follow your lead.

Communicating to influence is about understanding what your audience, stakeholders or clients need, then showing how the ideas you're proposing will meet those needs. Ideally it's about finding a win-win solution then communicating it with the right energy and emotion for your audience.

Communicating to influence is also about how you build your leadership brand and reputation. Every interaction people have with you – whether that's a late-night email, an all-staff Slack channel, a rushed arrival at the office or a hungover Monday morning – every interaction is influencing people.

If you are a natural Warrior or Monarch, Communicate to Influence is the skillset that probably comes most naturally to you. You're probably already good at pitching and may speak eloquently about your inspirational vision for your business. You probably have one or two influencing superpowers, but as your business grows and what it requires of you as a founder changes, you will need to refine and enhance these skills so they can adapt to multiple influencing challenges with multiple types of stakeholders. You'll need to be as effective when you appear on stage or in the media as you are when you're pitching to a client. You'll need to have as much impact when you're presenting to a group or proactively influencing your board as you do when pitching your business to investors or clients.

If this style of communication doesn't come naturally to you, it will take effort and discipline to grow your influencing skills and muscles. But your business needs you to get good at this – so get cracking!

A lot of founders I coach fall into one or two typical influencing traps:

- They pitch into submission, whatever the problem is
- They bombard people with too much or irrelevant information
- They're great at influencing when they're trying to win something (a new client, an investment) then ignore their influencing responsibilities when it comes to business as usual (inspiring the team on an on-going basis, proactively managing the board or investors)
- They forget about the importance of their personal brand

To influence effectively as you grow your business, there are some core principles of the Communicate to Influence style that you need to know:

- The 5Ps model
- The Influence Mindset formula
- The 4Cs of building your leadership brand

Once you understand these core principles, you'll be able to diagnose where you may be stumbling, and what to do about it.

Core principles of the Communicate to Influence style

1. The 5Ps model

To demystify and master the art of influence you first need to understand how people make decisions.

When I first started researching the art of influence fifteen years ago, I was overwhelmed with the amount of information available on the subject. It was only when I read about the art of copywriting that the penny dropped.[8] Copywriters are

---

8   R Bly, *The Copywriter's Handbook* (Henry Holt, 2013)

fascinated by what needs to happen for a person to shift from 'Never heard of that product' to 'I want it', and they apply a scientific 'test and measure' approach to find out the answer. Their work sits at the intersection of psychology and sales, and I used it to create the 5Ps model of influence, which I have shared with every founder I have coached since.

The 5Ps model applies whenever you want to influence anyone to do anything. Use it when you need to:

► Write a pitch

► Prepare for a key presentation

► Influence a team

► Create new sales materials

► Navigate a complicated sale

► Get ready for an important meeting

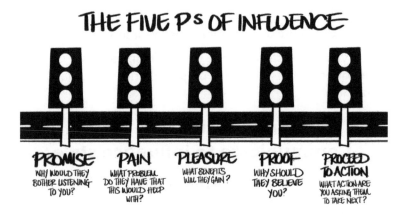

THE FIVE Ps OF INFLUENCE

PROMISE WHY WOULD THEY BOTHER LISTENING TO YOU?

PAIN WHAT PROBLEM DO THEY HAVE THAT THIS WOULD HELP WITH?

PLEASURE WHAT BENEFITS WILL THEY GAIN?

PROOF WHY SHOULD THEY BELIEVE YOU?

PROCEED TO ACTION WHAT ACTION ARE YOU ASKING THEM TO TAKE NEXT?

This model shows the steps you need to guide people through if you're going to move them from ambivalence to buy-in. Think of each step as a set of traffic lights that need to turn green.

P1 – Promise

First, you need to get your audience's attention. If you're influencing an individual or a team you've not met before, they have to agree to listen to you in the first place. If you are influencing a board, another team or an existing client, they must be engaged and eager to converse. If you're writing a proposal or presentation, you need to grab your readers' attention and keep it. Ask yourself: Why would my audience bother meeting me or listening to me? What's in it for them?

Make your answer to this the first thing your audience sees or hears. Show them why they should bother listening or reading further. Make your message pithy and intriguing if you can. Promise to make the time they spend on this worth their while.

For example, say you want to influence your sales team to engage with a new CRM. If you start a presentation by saying, 'Hi, thanks for your time today. I know how busy you are and won't keep you long. I'm going to talk today about widget software 5.0 and how it's better than widget software 4.0', you've already lost your audience. But if you say, 'You've told us how much time you're wasting each day on admin and procedure. We've listened. I'm going to share an idea that could save your sales team 300 hours in wasted data-entry time in the next six months', they'll listen.

P2 – Pain (problem)

Once you have an audience's attention, they will keep paying attention if they believe you can help them solve a problem they're having. You need to speak to their pain.

For example: 'The existing CRM is clunky, and it doesn't allow you to cross-reference in the way you need. You are spending more time on data entry than you are on the phone with clients. It's getting in the way of you achieving your sales targets and I know how important those are to you.'

Communicating to influence is about understanding how people form impressions and make decisions, then adapting your communication in line with that.

P3 – Pleasure (benefit)

Next, you need to clarify the benefits to the audience of making the decision you are asking them to make. Emphasise the pleasure they will derive from adopting your idea.

For example: 'You want to spend less time on data entry and more time serving your clients. You need software that is simple and gives you critical insights into your clients and sales opportunities. If we give you fast access to crucial client data, and free up 300 hours of your team's time in the next six months, imagine what you could achieve instead.'

P4 – Proof

Next, you need to show your audience how you/your idea/your product/your company is the right one to enable them to get from pain to pleasure. Here you want to share just enough information to build their confidence. You may be super-excited about all the whizzy technical elements of your idea, but it's unlikely your audience is. Just share what they care about.

For example: 'Widget software 5.0 is used by [x] and [y] companies. It removes six steps in the data-entry process and it allows you to compare [a] with [b], so you can identify new opportunities for sales. We've beta tested it with team [z] and they found individuals saved on average three hours a week.'

P5 – Proceed to action

Finally, you need to move from influence to action. Now that your audience is at the front door of your idea, invite them in and let them know where to go.

For example: 'To progress things, I need two members of the sales team to work with IT to help us scope a transition plan.'

2. The Influence Mindset Formula

The 5Ps tells you how to craft an influential message, but it is only one side of the influencing coin. We've all been sold to by people we don't like or don't trust, people who we immediately know are self-serving, regardless of their sales patter. Brilliant influencers know that relationship, trust and rapport are as important as the message. The 5Ps tells you *what* to do to influence an audience, but the *how* and *why* are equally important. Brilliant influencers anchor their *how* in rapport and relationships and their *why* in service and a win-win mindset.

The Influence Mindset = Belief + Service + Curiosity

Belief

To be an effective influencer, you must have belief in your idea. If you're trying to sell an idea you don't really believe in, that will come across. Even with the most polished and practised sales patter, your audience will know that something is off.

Service

When influencing, you need to anchor yourself in a service mindset. Your message should be grounded in the needs and aspirations of your audience, and your intention rooted in service to them. There's little as unattractive as a self-serving leader trying to manipulate their audience to their own selfish ends.

Curiosity

To be a good influencer, you need to be enormously curious. You need to put yourself in your audience's shoes if your message and delivery is going to resonate for them.

When I start work with a new founder I'll often ask them to pitch me their business, or I'll listen in as they present in a team or stakeholder meeting. Here's how poor influencers spend their time:

Poor Influencers = 90% Belief + 5% Service + 5% Curiosity

Poor influencers spend most of their time focusing on their own brilliant idea, and little time being curious about what their audience needs or how they can be of service to them. Their presentations are front-loaded with data and proof points, without even mentioning why their audience should care. They ignore the Promise, Pain and Pleasure elements of the 5Ps, all of which require curiosity and a service mindset. They present information that they think is interesting, rather than the information their audience cares about, and they do this in a way that puts their audience to sleep.

On the other hand, when you listen to a pitch or presentation from a brilliant influencer, here's how they're spending their time:

Brilliant Influencers = 15% Belief + 15% Service + 70% Curiosity

Brilliant influencers spend a huge amount of time being curious about their audience, and they use what they discover to craft messages that really land. When you ask them afterwards how they prepared for the presentation, talk or meeting, they'll tell you that they've been thinking about their stakeholders' worlds, needs and drivers. Brilliant influencers ask themselves questions like:

- What's keeping my audience up at night?
- What do they care about?
- How do my audience like to communicate?
- What would make this idea a win for them?
- How is our rapport?
- How strong is my authority to act?
- How much buy-in and engagement do I have?

It's obvious why curiosity is so important when you think about the 5Ps model above. It's only when you've spent enough time understanding why your audience would care (Promise), the challenges they have that your idea can solve (Pain), and what would make your idea a big win for them (Pleasure), that they will care whether your idea is a good one (Proof) and consider taking action (Proceed). All of that is only effective if you've spent enough time genuinely caring about your audience and building rapport with them.

3. Building your leadership brand

As your business grows from start-up to scale-up to grown-up, your communication becomes increasingly less direct. As your audience grows, and you look to influence hundreds, if not thousands, of people (employees, customers, stakeholders), the degree to which you are able to inspire followership will rely on your leadership brand and reputation. People will look to you as a source of credibility, trust and inspiration, so your leadership brand becomes as important as any direct communication.

While the 5Ps model draws much from the art of copywriting and sales, your leadership brand draws from the world of marketing. The first thing a brand marketing firm will do when they start work with a new company is understand the brand's core values and a product's unique selling point (USP). They then decide which channels they are going to use to communicate these key messages with their audience. Your leadership brand approach is the same.

There are four steps you need to follow.

Step 1: Understand your current leadership brand

Get a clear idea of what your leadership brand currently is, for either good or ill. If you don't have an employee feedback survey to tell you this, ask five people who know you well to give you the unvarnished truth about your current reputation.

Step 2: Clarify your leadership USP

You need to be clear on what your leadership unique selling point (USP) is and how you can hone and develop it. Maybe you're the tech wizard or the visionary, the political genius or the caring parent. Maybe you're the no-BS straight-shooter or the innovative creative source. Once you have a sense of the kernel of your USP, think about how you can develop and grow that in service of the business's objectives.

Step 3: Decide which brand values you would like to be known for

Imagine overhearing people talking about you in two years' time. How would you like them to describe you as a founder? Do you want them to say that you are considered, impactful and have grace and poise? Or would you like them to say you are dynamic, powerful, visionary and inspiring? What four adjectives would you like them to use to describe you?

Step 4: Choose your communication channels

With a clear sense of your leadership USP and brand values, you can explore the channels you will use to communicate these. Consider internal channels like Slack, town halls, all-staff comms, and external channels like social media, press, TV, events and talks. Never forget that one of the strongest channels you have is simply how you walk around the office. Keep cool, dress appropriately for your leadership brand, put a smile on your face, and wear your invisible crown.

CASE STUDY: MARK

Mark was a researcher at a prestigious university when he realised his work had huge applications in the manufacturing industry.

He and his business partner worked with an incubator at their university, launched their business, won a handful of anchor clients and built a core team. Mark was a rather dour scientist, uncomfortable on stage and more at home presenting academic research than pitch decks. The process he'd developed, however, was so compelling to clients that his influencing skills really weren't that important initially.

I was introduced to Mark by his lead investor when the company had grown to about forty people. His investor had concerns about how Mark was working with the board and had heard rumblings of discontent from a couple of clients and key members of the executive team. 'Mark is struggling to take the board with him,' the investor said. 'He's sullen and difficult in board meetings and clients complain that he's not listening to feedback or managing people's expectations well. He avoids telling us bad news, gets defensive when challenged, and he's losing people.'

It was immediately clear that Mark couldn't or wouldn't Communicate to Influence. I introduced him to the Influence Mindset formula and asked him what proportion of his conversations were centred in curiosity and service, and how much in belief in his idea.

'I'm about 95% belief in my idea with 5% curiosity,' he said.

We set out to think through the minimal viable influencing he could engage with to prevent the client, investor and staff problems that were affecting him. Board meetings were the biggest source of strain for Mark, so we looked at how the 5Ps could help. We explored what his investor's pains and aspirations were and how he could speak to those.

Mark developed a new way of preparing for and presenting to his board. He started to pre-align with key board members around contentious issues. He crafted presentations that followed the 5Ps model, and the huge data tables and academic information he favoured were relegated to their proper place (in pre-read decks or appendices).

He followed the same approach with critical client reviews and saw an immediate reduction in client complaints as he triangulated more and pre-empted problems. He used the same approach with his team. He shared an edited version of his board deck with his staff by way of a bi-annual company update and found that people were inspired by what he was sharing.

'I see it now as preventative medicine,' he said. 'Twice a year, I dive down into influencing, then everyone is dosed up on inspiration and confidence for the next six months, and they leave me alone to get on with the things I enjoy doing.'

Mark's company now has over 120 staff in four countries and we're beginning to explore questions around his leadership brand. Mark is a self-confessed mad scientist. Think overflowing desk, crazy hair and a distracted air. There's something endearing about it, but you wouldn't necessarily look at him in a business meeting and think, 'Yes, I trust this man to lead me into the future.' At the moment, Mark is faced with a choice of whether to move to the CTO role and let someone else step into the CEO role, or to embrace the CEO role and all that it requires. We're yet to see whether he uplevels his leadership brand from mad scientist to powerful CEO, or whether he stays happily in his technical realm. Either way, he's an extraordinary founder and is changing the world one manufacturing plant at a time.

What next?

Complete the Communicate to Influence self-test. Then ask yourself: Given the challenges I'm facing and our stage of business, do I need to strengthen my Communicate to Influence skills?

If you do, focus on the exercises in the Communicate to Influence Toolbox, which contains exercises that will help you turn theory into practice. The Toolbox includes an exercise to help you prepare for any meeting where you want to increase your impact and influence, and an exercise to help you develop more personal presence. The Toolbox shows you how to use the 5Ps to craft influential messages and provides a guide to help you structure presentations for maximum impact. Last but not least, it includes some key pointers on how to influence your investors or board.

Communicate to Influence self-test	0 Very rarely	1 Rarely	2 Often	3 Very often
I am good pitching				
I am good at selling				
I am good at influencing one-to-one				
I am a good presenter				
I communicate my leadership brand				
I am a strong public speaker				
I am good at influencing one to many				
I understand how to manage stakeholders				
I think about what my audience needs from me				
I put myself in my audience's shoes				
I talk about benefits not functions				
I can read a room				
I avoid presenting huge amounts of irrelevant detail				
My decks only contain information that can't be shared verbally or in pre-reads or appendices				
I know what my audience cares about				
I think about how, not just what, to communicate				
I think about rapport levels before making a big ask				

Communicate to Influence self-test	0 Very rarely	1 Rarely	2 Often	3 Very often
I reflect on how much authority I have to act				
I triangulate with stakeholders				
I think about my leadership reputation				
I know what I want to be known for				
People know what I stand for as a leader				
I make use of nonverbal communication				
I understand how to manage my board / investees				
I build a coalition for new ideas before I present them				
Column totals: (Score 1 for rarely, 2 for often, 3 for very often)				
Add your column scores together to give you your **Communicate to Influence score:**				

Your Communicate to Influence score

If you scored 60–75: Congratulations, you have mastered the Communicate to Influence style. Feel free to jump to the next section.

If you scored 40–59: You have mastered some of the key Communicate to Influence skills. Look at the Communicate to Influence Tools in the Toolbox to see which skills you may need to strengthen.

If you scored 0–39: You need to strengthen your Communicate to Influence skills. Prioritise the exercises in the Communicate to Influence Tools in the Toolbox.

Part Two Summary: The Two Communication Styles And How To Master Them

To survive as a founder of a scaling business you need to be able to Communicate to Manage and Communicate to Influence.

At the start-up stage you need to Communicate to Influence one-to-one, in pitches and sales. At the scale-up stage you also need to Communicate to Manage individuals and teams. At the grown-up stage you also need to Communicate to Influence one to many and Communicate to Manage stakeholders and leadership brand.

Core principles of communicating to manage

- ▶ Craft clarity (on the 4Rs – role, rules, results and review)
- ▶ Adopt the Manage Mindset (brave + kind + clean)
- ▶ Stay out of the Drama Triangle

Core principles of communicating to influence

- ▶ Use the 5Ps model of influence
- ▶ Remember the influence formula (belief + service + curiosity)
- ▶ Build your leadership brand

Questions to ask yourself

► Which is your preferred communication style – managing or influencing?

► Are you happiest one-to-one or one-to-many?

► Are you happiest participating or presenting?

► How well suited is your preferred communication style to the stage of business you're at and/or the challenges you're currently facing?

► Which communication style do you most need to strengthen?

The Toolbox

In the Toolbox at the end of this book you will find a series of exercises that will help you grow Communicate to Manage and Communicate to Influence skills:

Communicate to Manage tools

1. Give good feedback using clean language
2. Coach for performance
3. Create a team charter
4. Introduce a team process review
5. Manage team dynamics

Communicate to Influence tools

1. Think before you meet
2. Use the 5Ps to prepare for key communications
3. Structure your communication for maximum impact
4. Develop personal presence
5. Manage your investors or board

PART THREE

SELF-MASTERY

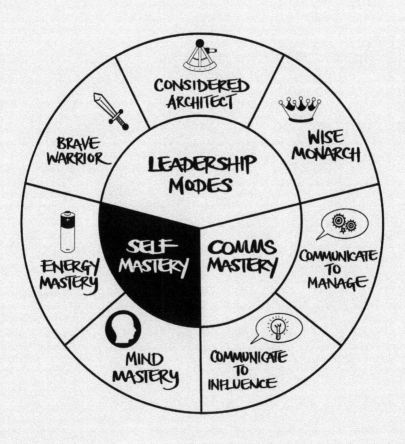

An Introduction To Self-Mastery

I met Angelo shortly after he secured a $25m investment for his tech start-up. Angelo had an IQ in the high 170s, a PhD from Oxford University, a brilliant idea for a start-up in an exploding field and a magical ability to convince people to join him on his quest. VCs were lined up to invest in his company, but within a couple of months of closing the funding round, cracks began to show. Angelo was referred to me after the company lost three of its four anchor clients within six months of the close, and one senior team member walked out and sued the company.

I often start work with a founder with a one-month round of diagnostics. I interview key staff, investors and advisors, and complete a set of psychometric assessments, to help me understand exactly where we need to focus our work. During the diagnostic phase with Angelo, I was perplexed. He was charm personified in his conversations with me and played down the challenges the business was facing. His team, all less than six months in the business, told me that, while they hadn't seen much of Angelo recently as he'd been travelling, they found him an inspiring and energising leader. They felt he was probably too stressed, and hoped I would help him manage his overwhelm, but there were no massive red flags. I left the interviews impressed at Angelo's ability to pull together such a smart, engaged and committed team. Why, then, had three anchor clients and his lead developer all jumped ship?

In the second month of coaching, things became clearer. Emails arrived from Angelo at 1, 2 or 3am, then I wouldn't hear from him for a week before a flurry of WhatsApp messages arrived, as many as seven in ten minutes, all demanding an urgent response. As he got to know me better, he let his best behaviour slip, and he shifted from pitching me his vision to complaining about everybody and everything. His mood swung wildly. One moment he was inspired, energised and able to leap tall buildings in a single bound, with a product and team he was proud of. The next moment, he was resentful, bitter, aggressive and 'surrounded by idiots and a shit product'.

Angelo's problem was that he had absolutely no self-mastery. His emotional and physical energy swung wildly and his ability to lead swung with them. While his IQ was through the roof, his EQ – his emotional intelligence – was on the floor. He didn't know how to manage his emotions or his psychological needs, and when he couldn't solve a problem with an algorithm, he bounced between charm and despair, people-pleasing and seething resentment. He slept sporadically, lived on a diet of Deliveroo and coffee, and by the end of each workday was so wired that the only way he could relax was by drinking alcohol or by smoking copious amounts of weed. He was stuck in a vicious cycle where the solutions he was using to manage his mood (comfort food, booze and weed) were leaving him so physically tired and wrung out, that he felt worse, not better.

The two elements of self-mastery

Scaling a business can be relentless and challenging. Combine an SAS obstacle course and an ultramarathon and you have a pretty good idea of what it takes. Resilience is key. At few other times is so much required of a founder CEO than in the scale-up stage of business. You need to dial between Brave Warrior, Considered Architect and Wise Monarch leadership modes multiple times a day, while maintaining your integrity and building a team who allow you to play from your strengths.

To survive and thrive
as a founder, you
need to show up
as the best version
of yourself, and
Self-mastery is a
precondition of that.

You need to manage a whole panoply of personalities, teams and relationships – one moment communicating to influence, the next communicating to manage. You cannot do any of that if you're full of resentment, anger or despair, or if you are physically and emotionally worn out because you're pulling eighteen-hour days or have a prodigious hangover.

While Parts One and Two of this book were about the skills you need to develop to thrive as a founder, Part Three is about the personal foundation you need to build to effectively deploy those skills. There is no point honing your Considered Architect leadership style if you still suffer from extreme mood swings or are prey to an overly negative mindset. It's equally futile mastering influencing or feedback skills if you are so physically and mentally exhausted that you can't effectively put those skills to use.

In the next chapters, we'll look at the two key elements to self-mastery:

1. Mind Mastery

2. Energy Mastery

With Mind Mastery, we explore:

▸   Negative thoughts and beliefs, what happens when they're triggered and how to hack them

▸   Ego needs and fears, what happens when we're gripped by them, and how to get out from under them

With Energy Mastery, we look at how to:

▸   Maintain healthy levels of physical, emotional and mental energy

▸   Manage healthy levels of stress

Without this self-mastery, at best, you'll be a hostage to your own negative beliefs, mood and mindset, and at worst, you'll blow your business up in a fit of pique or a self-sabotaging blaze of glory.

We'll look at a few simple but powerful concepts and a framework for self-mastery, which will help ensure that you are running the show, rather than being run by your frustration, resentment, compulsive behaviour or exhaustion. It will also show you how to take care of your physical energy so that you can continue to run the scale-up marathon effectively and healthily, rather than crash out exhausted after mile five.

7

Mind Mastery

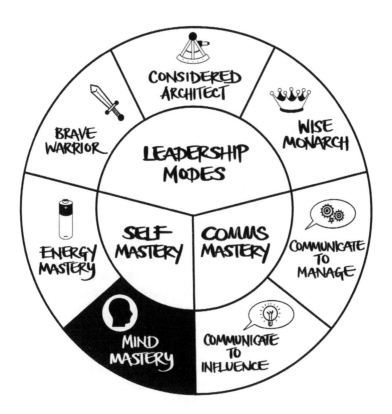

We've all had the experience of knowing what we should do, then doing the opposite, despite our best intentions. We sit at the end of a day and wonder:

- ► Why did I procrastinate on that important task today?

- ► Why did I get so nervous in that meeting?

- ► Why did I lose my temper?

- ► Why didn't I speak up/shut up?

- ► Why can't I just get along with Bob/Mary?

The purpose of this chapter is to answer those questions and to give you tactics for mastering your mindset and mood so you can create different outcomes.

Your mind is like an iceberg with over 90% of it working below the level of your conscious awareness.[9] That's an alarming fact. It means that you are not directly aware of the large majority of what your brain tells you to do. That's great when it comes to physical processes like regulating your heartbeat or triggering stomach acids to digest food. When it comes to the fears, beliefs and assumptions we hold, and the mistakes we habitually make because of them, it's less great. None of us wants to repeat the same mistakes we've made over and over again like an automaton. Instead, we need to bring as much of that subconscious processing as possible to the surface so that we can do something about it.

The brain is made up of neural pathways, connections between neurons, that have been laid down over time. Think of the word 'donkey' for a moment. What associations does your brain make for you? My immediate thoughts are grey and seaside. Those are the neural pathways that have been laid down

9   G Markowsky, 'Physiology', Britannia (no date), www.britannica.com/science/information-theory/Physiology, accessed 10 May 2022

by my previous experience. Those are the strongest associations my brain makes for me, so I've obviously made those connections quite a few times – those pathways are like neural superhighways, the well-driven motorways of my brain. If I think a little longer about the word 'donkey', my brain starts to travel down its less commonly travelled neural side roads, and I think about animal sanctuaries and Mister Ed. Here's where my brain starts playing tricks on me. Because my first thought was 'grey', my brain has leapt to an image from a black-and-white TV show called *Mister Ed*, but Mister Ed was actually a horse. And it hasn't brought up the memory of Shrek's Donkey or Eeyore, both of whom are more famous donkey characters. My first thought 'grey' has sent my subconscious off on an incorrect tangent.

Our subconscious brain makes incorrect assumptions and takes shortcuts, and for the sake of cognitive ease, it takes us down well-trodden habitual neural motorways. Your brain is wired with millions of neural pathways of belief, assumption, habit and need, born from your formative experience, the culture you grew up in and your personal narrative. Your beliefs about other people, about yourself, about what is good and bad, about what to fear and what to desire, have all been laid down as neural superhighways in your subconscious brain.

Earlier in this book, I gave the analogy of the tennis player who needs to be able to play a variety of shots to become a champion. So far, we've talked about the variety of techniques you need to master in order to survive and thrive as a founder. Imagine our championship founder out on centre court confidently playing all their different shots, assured of victory. They shift between Brave Warrior, Considered Architect and Wise Monarch modes, and they Communicate to Influence and to Manage with ease.

Now let's bring in the subconscious mind with all its needs, fears, beliefs and emotions. What happens when the tennis player gets angry with the umpire, or their opponent puts them off their stride with some gamesmanship? What happens if they start to relive a previous loss to their opponent, or begin to stress about what will happen if they lose this rally? Our player is immediately off their game. So, too, is our championship founder.

Millions of pages have been written about the mind and all its subconscious vagaries. Here, we'll look at two of the subconscious processes that most commonly block success and inhibit founders from playing their A-game: ego needs and negative beliefs.

Ego needs and how to hack them

We all understand what it feels like to have an unmet physical need. If you're thirsty, hungry or tired, that unmet need for fluid, food or sleep will hijack you until it's met. You could be in the most beautiful place in the world, on a once-in-a-lifetime sightseeing trip, but if you need the toilet, all you will be able to think about is finding one. That need will hijack you until it's met. Only then will you be able to take in the splendour of your surroundings.

Ego needs act in the same way. Here we use the word 'ego' as Freud intended it, not to describe a sense of self-importance, but to describe the part of the mind that mediates between the conscious and the subconscious and is the seat of your personal identity. Your subconscious is programmed with a set of things it thinks it needs to be safe. We'll call these ego needs. Ego needs are established in your formative years and/or as a result of traumatic experiences, and are reinforced through the repeated choices you make in adult life.

Let's take an example of a founder who has an ego need for freedom. Perhaps this stems from a childhood where they were constantly frustrated by the things their parents or siblings wouldn't let them do. Our founder's subconscious has built a connection: lack of freedom is something that causes frustration and should be avoided at all costs. Unsurprisingly as an adult, they've made lots of choices that positively reinforce the belief that they need freedom. Whenever their freedom is compromised, negative emotions bubble up because this is, for the subconscious brain, something to be feared.

"

Mind Mastery
ensures that your
business is run by
you, not by your
subconscious fears
and ego needs.

"

Now this founder is running a company and the business needs them to follow a strategic plan, facilitate regular leadership team meetings, and take counsel from team members and investors. But our freedom-needing founder feels a little hot under the collar. Their ego need has been triggered and their frustration, anxiety and resentment increase. 'Why do all these people need stuff from me?' they ask. 'Don't they realise I work at my best when I'm left to do my own thing?'

Suddenly the needs of the organisation and the ego needs of the founder are at odds. The founder is off their game and the leadership team aren't getting what they need to succeed. Unless the founder can bring these subconscious processes to the surface and master them, the ego need that began in childhood will hijack their business.

The need–fear–shadow cycle

Ego needs, unlike physical needs, are not genuine survival needs, but they feel like they are. We need water, food and sleep to survive. We don't actually need power, justice, approval or freedom to stay alive, but when those ego needs are triggered, it can feel like we're in a life-or-death situation.

When we feel fear or other negative emotions like frustration, resentment or anger, we are bounced out of our rational mind and into a set of shadow thoughts and behaviours. These shadows are unhelpful ways of thinking and acting that we have developed as survival mechanisms over our lifetime. Perhaps we bounce into people-pleasing and approval-seeking, or into aggression and argumentativeness. Perhaps we are bounced into overworking or overpromising, into isolating or avoiding, or into judging or overcriticising.

The problem is that these shadow thoughts and behaviours typically net us the exact thing we were afraid of and get us the very opposite of what we need. In the past twenty years, I've seen this process play out so many times, I've given it its own name: the need–fear–shadow cycle.

THE NEED-FEAR-SHADOW CYCLE

Let's take two examples. Imagine that through your formative years you developed an ego need for approval. You're about to meet with a group of disgruntled investors who are worried about the performance of your company. Your subconscious is on high 'approval-need' alert and you're feeling disproportionate amounts of anxiety and dread. Your shadow behaviours kick in. You've avoided thinking about the meeting, but now it's here, you people-please and try to charm your way out of it. You deflect difficult questions and put on the 'there's no problem here' jazz-hands show. But for the investors looking for answers, this approach doesn't cut it, and you get more disapproval than approval.

Or let's imagine you have an ego need for authority, power or control. You see that a member of your leadership team has done something that you don't like and that they didn't check with you. Your need for control is triggered and along come anger, frustration and resentment. Your shadow behaviours and patterns of thinking kick in, and you berate the person in a team meeting or immediately pull the task back and do it yourself. Is that person more likely to seek your counsel in the future, or less?

Time and again, these subconscious patterns of unmet needs, negative emotions and shadow behaviours play out, leaving both you and your business with less and less of what you need. To survive and thrive as a founder, you need to understand your ego needs and your shadow behaviours so you can break this cycle. You must manage your subconscious processes, or you will continue to be hijacked by them.

Hacking the need–fear–shadow cycle

If you want to understand where your deeply held fears and psychological needs come from, see a therapist. If you want a super-quick hack to get out from under them, try a simple, though not easy, three-step process:

▶ **Step 1:** Understand your top three core psychological needs.

▶ **Step 2:** Understand your top five shadow patterns of behaving and thinking.

▶ **Step 3:** Every time you spot your ego needs being triggered, do the exact opposite of your shadow patterns.

In the Toolbox at the back of this book, you'll find exercises to help you identify your needs, shadows and their opposites. For the moment, though, just hold onto one critical, deceptively simple concept – when you are frustrated, resentful or fearful, do the opposite of what you want to do.

For example:

▶ If you want to shout, ask questions.

▶ If you want to people-please, have a tough conversation.

▶ If you want to self-isolate, talk to someone.

▶ If you want to gossip, keep your counsel.

▶ If you want to micromanage, coach.

▶ If you want to judge, seek to understand.

I'm not suggesting you become a saint – more a badass Buddha. There are as many times you'll need to be tough, brave and direct as there are to be forgiving, understanding and tolerant. But when you're hijacked by ego needs and fear it's a pretty good bet that the best course of action is to do the opposite of what you want to do. Once you've identified your own shadow behaviours using the exercise at the back of the book, it will be crystal clear how these exacerbate the problems you're trying to solve or make it difficult to get your needs met. For the moment, though, let's look at examples of what happens when we try the 'do the opposite' approach.

Remember the approval-seeking founder with the disgruntled investors? Imagine that instead of avoiding or charming or manipulating, they walk into the meeting and address the bad news directly, honestly and with integrity. They talk appropriately to their audience about the business's challenges and their strategy for managing them. The investors feel reassured that the founder understands their concerns, trusts them and has a plan. Our founder ends up with more approval, not less.

Now let's turn to the founder with the core need for control, whose team member did not consult him on an important decision. Instead of getting angry or micromanaging, our founder does the opposite and tries to understand. They speak with their team member calmly and get curious about the decision that person made. If necessary, they implement a new protocol for agreeing important decisions moving forward. Our founder ends up with more control, not less.

This is a deceptively simple approach to managing your ego needs and fears, but it requires real effort and courage. The first time you try to do the opposite, your ego is going to scream at you, 'This won't work! But that's not fair/right! What if [x] or [y] happens?' That will be your ego trying to protect you from what it perceives to be an imminent threat. When this happens to you – and it will – you have to decide you want to be successful and effective *more* than you want to be right, have control or be approved (or whatever your ego need demands). You have to push through this fear-induced self-talk with courage and do the opposite anyway.

Once you've tried this a couple of times and realised that it's netting you more of what your ego needs not less, the resistance lessens and doing the opposite gets easier. I've been practising this approach for many years now and I still get it wrong sometimes. But then I remember that perfectionism and self-criticism are two of my shadow behaviours, so I'll do the opposite and have a little laugh at myself, say 'Bless me', and try to do better the next time.

The negative belief cycle

While fears and negative emotions bounce you into shadow behaviours that become self-sabotaging, beliefs and negative assumptions can play out in a similarly unhelpful fashion. Again, our subconscious brain is designed to make decision-making and information-processing easier and quicker, so it uses a collection of cognitive short cuts to speed things up. We process information through hard-wired neural pathways of habitual thinking, established by our previous experiences. This is helpful when you are making a cup of tea or doing the school run but becomes less helpful when you are trying to solve a complex interpersonal problem or dig your way out of a challenging situation.

Your beliefs are the pre-set filters you have about a situation or a person. They influence how you interpret your experiences and trigger a self-fulfilling cycle that simply reaffirms your beliefs. This cycle can be particularly insidious when it comes to the judgements you make about other people.

Let's take a situation where a member of your leadership team texts you just before an important meeting to tell you they can't attend. First, assume this is a person you admire, respect and trust. Let's call them Ben.

Ben texts to say he can't attend the meeting and you view this behaviour through your positive belief about him. You text back with, 'I hope you're OK! Don't worry, I've got this. I'll call you after the meeting. Let me know if you need anything from me.'

Ben feels supported and understood. After the meeting, you check in with each other. If there's a major problem, you work collaboratively to explore how to avoid that in the future. Your relationship and your working partnership are enhanced.

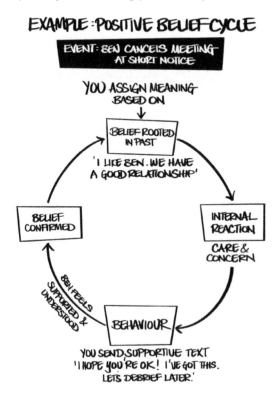

EXAMPLE : POSITIVE BELIEF CYCLE

EVENT: BEN CANCELS MEETING AT SHORT NOTICE

YOU ASSIGN MEANING BASED ON

BELIEF ROOTED IN PAST
'I LIKE BEN. WE HAVE A GOOD RELATIONSHIP'

BELIEF CONFIRMED

INTERNAL REACTION
CARE & CONCERN

BEN FEELS SUPPORTED & UNDERSTOOD

BEHAVIOUR
YOU SEND SUPPORTIVE TEXT 'I HOPE YOU'RE OK! I'VE GOT THIS. LETS DEBRIEF LATER.'

Now let's repeat that cycle with someone you hold negative beliefs about. Let's call them Bob.

Bob, who you don't like or trust, texts to say he can't attend an important meeting that's about to start. You view this through your negative belief about him. You roll your eyes and think, 'Typical.' You send a one-word text back saying, 'Fine.' You feel resentful. You don't bother to debrief with Bob afterwards.

You speak to a couple of your allies about how bloody unreliable Bob is. You feel validated.

Bob either thinks you genuinely meant his actions were fine, or he feels excluded and misunderstood. You don't have a conversation about how to solve the problem moving forward. Your negative belief about Bob is reaffirmed and your relationship and collaboration with him worsens.

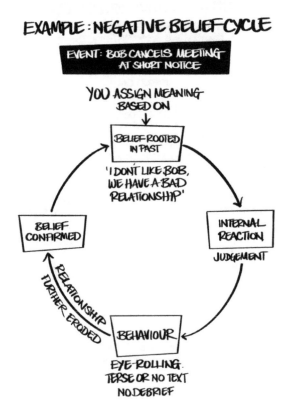

EXAMPLE : NEGATIVE BELIEF CYCLE

EVENT: BOB CANCELS MEETING AT SHORT NOTICE

YOU ASSIGN MEANING BASED ON

BELIEF ROOTED IN PAST

'I DON'T LIKE BOB, WE HAVE A BAD RELATIONSHIP'

INTERNAL REACTION

JUDGEMENT

BELIEF CONFIRMED

RELATIONSHIP FURTHER ERODED

BEHAVIOUR

EYE-ROLLING. TERSE OR NO TEXT NO DEBRIEF

The only difference between these two examples is the belief you are holding about the person involved.

To understand how this negative cycle operates, it's helpful to know about some of the short cuts and biases at work in our subconscious brain:

1. We have a confirmation bias, meaning we seek out evidence in line with our beliefs. This is why, for example, your choice of newspaper or news channel probably correlates with your political leaning.[10]

2. We dislike cognitive dissonance (eg holding two clashing data points), so we downplay evidence that is at odds with our beliefs or behaviours. This is why, for example, a person who is polishing off a bottle of wine each night but knows it's bad for them will downplay the behaviour to themselves as 'just a glass or two now and again'.[11]

3. Our brain has a reticular activating system, which ensures the conscious brain attends only to things it perceives to be relevant.[12] This is why, for example, we seem to hear our name more loudly when someone says it in a noisy room (the cocktail party effect). It's not that the person said our name more loudly, just that our brain registers it as relevant.

All these short cuts are essential to brain function, but they can get in the way of your effectiveness as a founder. The only way to prevent negative beliefs from becoming self-fulfilling negative cycles is to spot your beliefs and assumptions, and work hard to challenge or overcome them if they are unhelpful.

Luckily, the same cognitive short cuts that contribute to the problem also give us the solution to it. We can rewire an unhelpful negative belief by flooding our brains with information that contradicts it. If you consciously override the confirmation bias, the brain's dislike of cognitive dissonance kicks in, the reticular activating system starts filtering different information, and our beliefs start to shift.

---

10   R Nickerson, 'Confirmation bias: A ubiquitous phenomenon in many guises', *Review of General Psychology*, 2 (1998), pp175–220

11   L Festinger, *A Theory of Cognitive Dissonance* (Stanford University Press, 1957)

12   H Reinhold and MP West, 'Nervous System', in *Acute Care Handbook for Physical Therapists*, fourth edition (Elsevier, 2014) Available at www.sciencedirect.com/topics/medicine-and-dentistry/ascending-reticular-activating-system, accessed 11 May 2022

"

If you want to
understand where
your deeply held fears
and psychological
needs come from,
see a therapist.

If you want a super-
quick hack to get out
from under them,
use the exercises in
this chapter.

Imagine you are in a meeting and Mary says something that you disagree with. You don't like Mary much. She's very different from you and has made your life difficult in the past. At this point, you can either go down the well-trodden path of your negative belief cycle, or you can redirect your thinking down a more helpful route. Rather than rolling your eyes, cutting Mary off, then talking about her afterwards to your allies in the team, ask yourself: 'What would I do if I really cared about Mary? How could I work on our relationship to make it more positive and constructive? How would I behave if I decided to treat her as a human, not as an obstacle to my own desires and ambitions?'

You'll find that, as with the needs–fear–shadow cycle, you'll do the opposite of what your negative belief would tell you to do. You'll experience some internal resistance at first, but if you decide that you want to improve your relationship and outcomes with Mary, you have to push through it, remembering that the only thing that comes from the negative belief cycle is a self-fulfilling prophecy. If you want something to change, the only thing you can change is you.

It's not just our beliefs about other people that become unhelpfully self-fulfilling. Our negative beliefs about ourselves, about the world, about our business all risk becoming the reality our subconscious minds create. Think you're no good at public speaking? You'll avoid it or get nervous when you do it and reaffirm that belief. Think you can't maintain an entrepreneurial culture while building systems and processes? You'll never find a way to do it. Think your investors won't back a particular idea? You won't even try to build a convincing case to change their minds.

Hacking the negative belief cycle

Once you recognise how self-defeating many of your negative beliefs and assumptions are, you'll become more motivated to do the work to shift them. Luckily, as with the need–fear–shadow cycle, there's a simple three-step process for dismantling unhelpful negative beliefs:

- ▸ **Step 1:** Identify the unhelpful negative belief and how it's serving you.

- ▸ **Step 2:** Look for evidence to contradict the belief and/or find alternative explanations for the facts.

- ▸ **Step 3:** Act as if you believe the opposite.

Like the need–fear–shadow hack, this exercise is simple, but not easy. It's hard work to reprogramme a belief, and much easier to tread the well-worn negative neural superhighway in your brain.

It's also difficult to differentiate between facts and beliefs. Is it a fact that Bob is not right for that job, or that you're no good at managing a team, or are these just your negative beliefs? Facts are things you need to act upon: Bob may need replacing, or you may need to hire a chief of staff. Beliefs are things you need to challenge: you may need to behave differently around Bob or lean into your Communicate to Manage skills.

Let's go back to our example of Bob to see how this hack for the negative belief cycle works. You'll remember that Bob, who you don't like or trust, has missed an important meeting and you're rolling your eyes, thinking how typical this is and waiting for the opportunity to call an ally for a bit of watercooler Bob bitching.

Then you realise that you've jumped into a negative belief cycle and all this is going to do is give you more of the problem you have with Bob, not less. So you pause and decide to park your resentment until you have a moment to practise the three-step process above. That evening or weekend, you take a quiet moment to reflect and work through the questions of the three-step process:

Step 1 – Identify

What are my negative beliefs?

- Bob is untrustworthy.
- Bob is unreliable.
- I don't like Bob.
- I don't think Bob respects me.
- Bob is an arse.

How are these beliefs serving me?

- I feel morally superior.
- I don't have to make the effort, I can just blame him.
- I get to bond with my mates over our shared dislike of Bob.

Step 2 – Evidence

What evidence do I have to contradict my belief?

- Bob has a lovely wife, who must see something in him, so he can't be all bad.
- Bob does turn up to at least 80% of our meetings, so he's not always unreliable.
- Bob cares about his team and his people really like him, so he can't be a total arse.
- Bob is brilliant with clients.

Are there any alternative explanations for the facts?

- Perhaps Bob had a family or team crisis that he had to attend to, and that's why he missed the meeting.
- Perhaps Bob doesn't realise the impact of his no-show on me/others.
- Perhaps I haven't communicated my expectations clearly enough.
- Perhaps Bob knows I don't like him and has his own negative belief cycle playing out.

Step 3 – Act

What would I do if I believed the opposite?

If I believed Bob was a close friend and trusted partner and he'd missed a meeting:

- ▶ I'd check in and see if he was OK.
- ▶ I would be more curious and less judgemental.
- ▶ I would focus on solutions, not problems.
- ▶ My self-talk about Bob would be constructive rather than critical.
- ▶ I would remember that Bob is a human, with fears, doubts, ego needs and negative beliefs, just like me.
- ▶ I'd remember that I'm hardly a saint.

Having challenged your negative beliefs about Bob, what are you likely to do? In an earlier chapter, I said that, when faced with a problem, you have three rational options:

1. Accept the problem fully, with a peaceful heart.
2. Walk away from the problem.
3. Do something to change the problem – and the only thing you can ever change is what you say, think or do.

So, rather than rolling your eyes, ignoring Bob and gossiping at the watercooler, you'll either:

- ▶ Decide to let the problem go with a peaceful heart – it's not that important, or
- ▶ Respectfully exit him from the team if you genuinely believe that Bob's behaviour/attitude isn't going to change, or
- ▶ Ask Bob to go for a coffee and share your concerns and requests with him in a constructive and helpful manner (see the feedback process in the Toolbox)

Find a Mind Mastery buddy

You want your business to be run by the best version of you, not by fears and negative beliefs that were set down in your formative years and which are going to do little but net you more of what you don't want. You want your conscious mind running your business, not your subconscious fears and ego needs.

The challenge is that none of us see our subconscious processes clearly – after all, they are subconscious – and you may need to find a trusted buddy, mentor or coach to help you through this. I have a trusted mentor, Suki, whom I call whenever I think I may be believing my own hype. I've specifically asked her to challenge me and call me out on my negative thinking. I often dislike what she says, but she's almost always right.

I also have a coach whom I call when I'm in full-blown resentment or frustration. She's someone who knows my shadow behaviours and is skilled at spotting my negative beliefs at play. I've asked her to challenge me when she suspects I may have bounced into negative beliefs or assumptions. Again, I don't like what she says a lot of the time, but when my ego has deflated just a little, I'm always incredibly grateful for her challenges.

Who will you call upon to be your go-to Mind Mastery buddy?

What next?

Complete the Mind Mastery self-test. Then ask yourself: 'How might my ego needs or my negative beliefs be getting in the way of my ability to lead effectively?'

If you score low on the self-test, or know that your ego needs and beliefs are getting in the way, focus on the exercises in the Mind Mastery Toolbox. There you'll find an exercise to help you identify your own ego needs and shadow behaviours, as well as a tool to enable you to steer clear of them. The Toolbox also includes a simple five-step exercise to identify and dismantle unhelpful beliefs.

An important caveat

Mind Mastery hacks may not work if you are clinically depressed or anxious. If you think you are suffering from a mental health problem, do seek the advice of a professional.

Mind Mastery self-test	3 Very rarely	2 Rarely	1 Often	0 Very often
I find myself reliving things people have said				
If I think I have been treated unfairly, I feel resentful				
I get defensive when I think I'm being criticised				
I procrastinate				
I think I'm right				
I worry about making mistakes				
I gossip about people				
I get triggered				
I avoid difficult people, situations or problems				
I worry				
I plan for every eventuality				
I feel anxious if things aren't going right				
I complain				
I am a people-pleaser				
I get upset if people don't behave the way I think they should				
I overpromise				
If I have a negative belief, it's difficult to shake it				

Mind Mastery self-test	3 Very rarely	2 Rarely	1 Often	0 Very often
I have fears or regrets that get stuck in my mind				
I ruminate about things people have said or done				
I avoid uncomfortable conversations				
When I don't get the recognition I deserve, I get annoyed				
I struggle if I think my autonomy is threatened				
I need to feel in control				
I expect to be heard				
I get short-tempered and snappy				
Column totals: (Score 3 for very rarely, 2 for rarely, 1 for often)				
Add your column scores together to give you your **Mind Mastery score:**				

Your Mind Mastery score

If you scored 60–75: Congratulations, you have high levels of Mind Mastery. You are a badass Buddha! Skip to the next section.

If you scored 40–59: You are able to master your mind some of the time. Look at the Mind Mastery Toolbox for exercises to help you build more consistency.

If you scored 0–39: You need to strengthen your Mind Mastery. Prioritise the exercises in the Mind Mastery Toolbox.

8

Energy Mastery

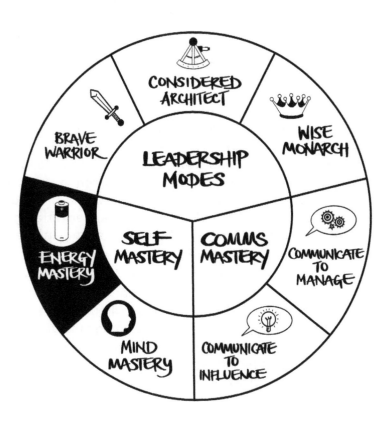

Stress, overwhelm and exhaustion are ubiquitous among founders. It's no surprise then that recent research identifies founder burnout as one of the top twenty reasons for the failure of VC-backed start-ups.[13] Even if you're not at risk of burnout, your levels of stress, overwhelm and exhaustion will negatively impact the quality and effectiveness of your leadership.

When I talk with founders about stress, I routinely hear things like, 'It'll be better when we've raised finance/got through the board meeting/hired a new COO.' The assumption seems to be that stress is a short-lived response to a transient external circumstance. But the reality is that, while the stressors may change, a founder's stress levels are likely to be constantly high for a significant period. Given that the average length of time from start-up to business sale is between six and ten years, you're likely to be dealing with high levels of stress for a long time.[14] Whatever your long-term plans or exit strategy may be, foundership is a marathon, not a sprint, and you need to stay race-fit throughout.

You want your business run by the best version of you and Energy Mastery is a precondition of that. Energy Mastery can't be something you try to squeeze in around the edges of your eighteen-hour work day if you're going to survive as a founder and genuinely give your business what it needs. Self-care has to come first, not last. If you put it first, everything else becomes first class.

---

13   CB Insights, 'The top 12 reasons why startups fail', CB Insights (2019), www.cbinsights.com/research-12-reasons-why-startups-fail, accessed 8 April 2022
14   S Abdullah, 'How long does it take a startup to exit?' Crunchbase (2018), https://about.crunchbase.com/blog/startup-exit, accessed 11 May 2022

If you want to survive and thrive as a founder, you can't afford to ignore the issue of self-care. Let's return to our analogy of the champion tennis player. They can have the best skills in the world, can have nailed the inner game of Mind Mastery, but if they're exhausted, hungover, stressed or burnt out, they're not going to win Wimbledon. The commercial landscape you operate in is incredibly competitive, just like the tennis player's grand slam tournament, and your ability as a founder to bring your energetic A-game will give you the competitive advantage you need to succeed.

You don't need me to tell you what great self-care looks like. I imagine you've been lectured at by partners, gym freaks and doctors alike. You know the benefits of a low-sugar/dairy/wheat diet, of drinking water, limiting caffeine and alcohol, getting good-quality sleep, regular exercise and practising meditation or mindfulness. I'm going to ask you to view self-care through a different lens. Rather than thinking of self-care as a list of 'shoulds' that you either resist or beat yourself up about, see them as a list of things that will either enhance or detract from your ability to play your A-game. This chapter includes ideas to help you stay at your peak and squeeze out every bit of competitive advantage possible.

In this chapter, we'll look at three approaches to Energy Mastery. Pick one and experiment with it for a month, then decide whether it works for you. If it does, and you find it helps you bring your A-game to work, keep it. If it doesn't, pick another approach and experiment with that instead. There's no one right way to master your energy – the only wrong way is not to do it at all.

The three energy tanks

A simple model to use when thinking about Energy Mastery is the three energy tanks. Imagine yourself with three tanks on your back, like the air tanks a diver would use. These three tanks represent your reserves of physical, mental and emotional energy.

"

Energy Mastery is about staying race fit for the founder marathon, not just the sprint.

"

At any time, you are either drawing on or refilling these reserves of energy through the activities you are engaged in. Certain activities deplete your reserves while others refill them.

The activities that will be most supportive for you will depend entirely on your unique personality, lifestyle and ambitions.

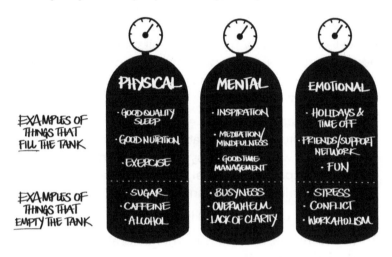

	PHYSICAL	MENTAL	EMOTIONAL
EXAMPLES OF THINGS THAT FILL THE TANK	· GOOD QUALITY SLEEP · GOOD NUTRITION · EXERCISE	· INSPIRATION · MEDITATION/ MINDFULNESS · GOOD TIME MANAGEMENT	· HOLIDAYS & TIME OFF · FRIENDS/SUPPORT NETWORK · FUN
EXAMPLES OF THINGS THAT EMPTY THE TANK	· SUGAR · CAFFEINE · ALCOHOL	· BUSYNESS · OVERWHELM · LACK OF CLARITY	· STRESS · CONFLICT · WORKAHOLISM

Let's take two highly successful founders I work with as examples. Chris is a gregarious, sporty thrill-seeker while Carrie is an elegant, refined Mayfair-dweller. Chris is at his best when he rides his high-performance bike three times a week and plans his next trek in Patagonia with his mates. Carrie is at her best when she has regular meditation sessions, massages, treatments and classes with a personal yoga teacher. Chris can cope fine with the odd glass of wine in the week. Carrie is much better when she doesn't drink at all. Chris drinks protein shakes and has a military regime of supplements. Carrie does a clean-eating detox twice a year. The only habit they share is that they are both religious about their morning routines and managing their diaries to keep them focused and effective.

Like Chris and Carrie, it doesn't matter what you do to manage your emotional, physical and psychological energy, so long as you do it. If you're more Krav Maga than mindful meditation, no problem. If you're more vindaloo curry than green juice – if it gives you good, consistent physical energy – who am I to argue with you? If you like to work all night and sleep till midday, that genuinely serves you, and you can set your business up to work like that, then go ahead.

Just make sure you're not giving yourself excuses for behaviours that actually mean you're not at your best. Be honest with yourself. Grow the habits and disciplines you need to put in your peak performance, and make sure you can do it for the marathon, not just the sprint. Adapt, explore, enjoy and be at your best.

If you're regularly running on empty, you can use the framework of the three tanks to create your own extreme self-care regime which will help you stay fit for the founder marathon. Think of your physical, mental and emotional energy tanks and ask yourself three questions:

1. On a scale of 1–10, how full is each tank?

2. For each tank, what activities or habits are most depleting for you?

3. For each tank, what activities or habits are most nourishing for you?

You can then use this information to move the dial on your self-care, in line with your preferences as a founder for either flexibility or planning. For example:

▶ If you like flexibility, use your answers to tweak your self-care on a weekly basis. Each week, do one more thing from the nourishing list and stop doing one thing from the depleting list.

▶ If you love a plan, take your answers and formulate a 3–6 month 'match-fit' plan for yourself.

The latter is the approach I favour, so once a quarter, I review my tanks, then make a plan for how to improve my nutrition, exercise and emotional self-care for the coming months. I might add in a juice fast or book some one-to-one sessions with a trainer. I might book a yoga retreat or sign up to a new meditation programme. Sometimes I'll add in a specific smart goal (eg lose 2 kg) or block chunks out of my diary to ensure I don't get too tired or rushed.

Whichever approach you choose, think of self-care as a separate workstream that needs as much attention as your financial systems, sales pipeline or top team. Without it, none of those will work for long anyway!

The stress-o-meter

Another framework you can use to think through your energy mastery is the stress-o-meter. Imagine you have an internal rev counter, like a rev counter on a car, that tracks your levels of stress, from 1 to 10. We all know what it sounds like when we rev a car too high for too long in the wrong gear. It gives us a warning sign that, if we continue to drive at 80 miles per hour in third gear, the engine is going to blow. Think of your internal stress-o-meter in the same way:

▶ When it's below 3, you are super-chilled.

▶ At a 4 or 5, the mind and body are revving normally and you're performing well.

▶ By the time you get to a 6 or 7 your mind is beginning to race, the adrenaline is pumping high, and you can feel the stress in your solar plexus.

▶ At 8 or 9, your mind is racing and you're asking if it's wine o'clock yet.

▶ If you get to 10, agggghhhhhhhhhh!

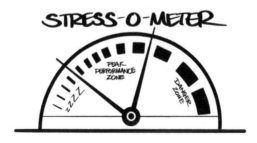

Many of us rev up to a level 7 or 8 without even noticing during the working day. We may start at a reasonable level, but after eight hours of relentless emails, calls, Zoom meetings, demands, questions and concerns, we're way up the stress-o-meter. If you find that the only way to slow your revs down after work is with a glass of wine, your engine is likely revving too hot.

Some of us become so accustomed to revving at a 7 or 8 that we actually get off on the adrenaline buzz. But as you move past about a 6 on your stress-o-meter, and your adrenaline and cortisol levels increase, it becomes increasingly difficult to manage your thoughts and behaviours, to practise considered leadership, to listen effectively and to respond powerfully.

Watch your stress levels for a day and notice what a 7 or 8 feels like. Maybe you have an ache in your chest, a knotted stomach, tense shoulders. Maybe you start getting short and impatient with everyone, or your mind races and can't settle to anything.

Identify the things that increase your revs. Lots of caffeine, not enough time between meetings, brooding on something that has happened or might happen, negative self-talk, running late or trying to do too much too fast are pretty typical rev increasers. Once you've identified them, think about how to reduce your revs. Here are a couple of ideas:

- **Cut back on caffeine:** When I started practising stress-o-meter rev management, the first thing I had to cut was caffeine – I simply couldn't keep below a 6 all day *and* drink coffee.

- **Pace the diary:** Leave ten minutes between meetings and limit the number of meetings you say yes to in a day. Schedule proper breaks for lunch.

- **Breathe:** Try the four-count breathing exercise: breathe in for the count of four; hold for the count of four; breath out for the count of four; hold for the count of four. Repeat this four times.

Whatever you discover about your own rev increasers and reducers, to survive and thrive through the founder marathon, you need to keep your revs below a 6. Your business, your team and your body will thank you.

Master the first hour of the day

A few years ago, I noticed that many of the thrusting Alpha CEOs I worked with in the US seemed to be in some sort of competition to see who could get up the earliest. Many of them quoted the book *The 5 AM Club* as a source of inspiration.[15] In the book, Robin Sharma suggests you wake up at 5am and spend twenty minutes exercising, twenty minutes meditating and twenty minutes reading or learning. The tagline of the book is: 'Own your morning. Elevate your life.'

While I find this approach a little too spartan, I agree with the premise. Your first waking hour sets the tone for the rest of your day. An hour of meditation, movement and reflection sets a very different tone from an hour of the snooze button and social media. It's a little like firing up your computer and deciding which programs you're going to run today – you are likely to operate at your best with ones that ground, support and energise you.

The most effective founders I coach have morning routines that super-charge them for the day ahead. Here are two examples from current clients:

▶ 'I wake at 6am, spend thirty minutes journaling and reflecting, fifteen minutes meditating and fifteen minutes planning my day. Then I take my vitamins, fill a two-litre bottle with enough mint leaves, lime and water to get me through the day and I'm ready for whatever life has in store. I try to do this religiously. If for any reason I miss it, I can really feel the difference by midday – and not in a good way.'

---

15   R Sharma, *The 5 AM Club: Own your morning. Elevate your life* (Harper Thorsons, 2018)

"

If you are an
ambitious and
goal-oriented
founder, the Energy
Mastery habit will
only kick in if you
genuinely believe
it's a precondition
for achieving your
goals. And it is.

"

▸ 'I get up an hour before the house wakes up. I read something like *The Daily Stoic* and spend a peaceful thirty minutes reflecting on my previous day and setting my intentions for the day ahead.[16] I go for a half-hour run with the dogs, then shower, have breakfast and am at my desk at 7am. I spend the first fifteen minutes at my desk reviewing my diary and setting my top three priorities for the day. Then I get going.'

A strong morning routine can become the foundation on which your founder success is established. Think for a moment about how you spend the first hour of the day. Are you creating a super-powered, strong foundation, or is it more slapdash and wobbly than it needs to be?

If your routine could be stronger, design one that fills your physical, mental and emotional energy tanks. Here are some elements you can include for each tank:

▸ **Physical** – stretching, exercising, taking vitamins, drinking hot water and lemon, eating a good breakfast, practising yoga, taking time for personal grooming, going for a run

▸ **Mental** – planning your day, journaling, learning, listening to insightful podcasts, making your bed

▸ **Emotional** – reading inspirational books/articles, practising meditation or visualisation techniques, praying, doing an evaluation of conscience, listening to music

Try your morning routine for two weeks, then decide whether to make it a permanent habit. If you do, refresh the routine every couple of months to stop it from getting stale.

---

16   R Holiday, *The Daily Stoic: 366 meditations on wisdom, perseverance, and the art of living* (Profile Books, 2016)

CASE STUDY: ISABELLE

Isabelle is the co-founder of a successful PR consultancy. She has a stellar reputation and an impressive roster of clients who would follow her to the ends of the earth.

Isabelle hired me a year after she'd bought out her co-founder, and coincidentally had separated from her long-term romantic partner.

'It's been an incredibly stressful eighteen months,' she said in our first call. 'My co-founder made the buy-out incredibly difficult and is now criticising us to everyone. In the meantime, I've been going through a break-up with my long-term partner who's being selfish and obnoxious. He knows what I'm going through at work, but still he's been insensitive and thoughtless, and just out for every dollar he can get out of the house sale.' Isabelle spoke incredibly fast, words coming out of her mouth at machine-gun pace, with barely a pause for breath.

Isabelle hired me to help her make the shift from co-founder to high-performance CEO, and we started coaching on the standard CEO topics: her vision, her leadership team, the culture of the organisation, etc. Honestly though, Isabelle didn't need a coach for any of that. She was a prodigious reader and an incredibly hard worker and could have done all that work on her own. It was obvious, though, that Isabelle was struggling to master herself. Her mind was either racing or full of resentment, while her physical energy and moods swung wildly.

As part of the onboarding process, I interviewed her top team. Her CFO captured the feedback best when he said, 'On a good day, Isabelle is one of the most extraordinary CEOs I've ever worked with, and on a bad day, she's the worst. The problem is, you never know if you're going to get good-day Isabelle or bad-day Isabelle.'

At our initial deep dive off-site we explored her shadow behaviours and needs. I gave her the list of shadow behaviours you'll find in the Toolbox at the end of this book and asked her to circle the words that represented her on a bad day. She circled 'insensitive', 'bossy', 'critical', 'controlling' and 'unkind'. I wrote those words up on a flipchart and asked her to imagine what it's like to be led by someone like that. As Isabelle looked at the flipchart, you could see all the bluster go out of her.

'Oh God,' she said. 'That's awful. That's not who I want to be as a CEO. I want to be inspiring, supportive and challenging. I want my company to be a brilliant place to work, and I want my team to be learning and growing. I care deeply about my team, but if that's the version of me they're experiencing, there's no way they'd know that.'

This uncomfortable insight gave Isabelle the impetus to look at the whole issue of self-mastery. We explored her ego needs and negative beliefs, the things that bounced her into resentment and stress. She saw how holding onto resentments about her former business partner and life partner were keeping her trapped in a negative self-fulfilling cycle. She realised that this cycle created such stress and psychological discomfort that she was throwing herself into work, wine or Netflix to escape her feelings. She hired a therapist to help her work through some of these negative feelings, and we switched the focus of our work to managing her energy.

Isabelle's stress-o-meter had been running at 8 for the past two years. She'd developed some unhelpful ways to manage it and had been living on adrenaline, caffeine and Chablis. 'I know I should meditate, go running, eat better and limit booze to the weekends but I don't have time, and I'm too exhausted at the end of each day to do anything about it,' she said.

I shared the analogy of the championship tennis player and asked, 'If you knew your success was 100% dependent on your ability to manage your energy, what would you do instead?'

Isabelle looked like I'd just pulled the rug out from under her, but she quickly developed a self-care plan. She put a fifteen-minute break between every meeting during the day and used diary software that meant her team couldn't add meetings at other times. Next she hired a personal trainer to come to her house at 6am, three days a week. Isabelle built in a nutrition hack and arranged to have a high-quality three-day juice fast delivered to her house once a month. Finally, she planned a series of mini-breaks and vacations. 'I know that if I have a break to look forward to every three months, then I'll be able to pace my energy.'

One year later, while Isabelle still sometimes trips into adrenaline and stress, her good days now significantly outweigh her bad. Turnover is up 20% and employee engagement up 7%. 'I still have a tendency to work too long and collapse into Netflix and chocolate at the end of the day. The difference now is I can see the link between my self-care and my effectiveness as a boss,' Isabelle said. 'Self-care is something I have to put first if I'm going to be the CEO I want to be. I can see the results, and I know that's because I am more consistent and dependable. I'm dealing with problems in a more effective way when they arise and our work for clients is better. If I have to give up sugar and Chablis, and meditate ten minutes a day to get those outcomes, I'll take that.'

What next?

Complete the Energy Mastery self-test. Then ask yourself: 'How might my low energy or high stress levels be getting in the way of my ability to lead effectively?'

If you score low on the self-test, or know that self-care and stress management are going to be important elements of your founder survival journey, focus on the exercises in the Energy Mastery Toolbox at the back of the book. There you'll find more on how to manage your three energy tanks and your stress-o-meter, as well as guidance on how to use your diary to manage your energy. The Toolbox also contains a brief guide to how to trigger your parasympathetic nervous system to help you manage your energy and stress.

An important caveat

There's a fine line between poor habits and compulsive or addictive behaviours. If you find that you simply cannot change some of your habits around work, food or drink, you may need to explore whether you've crossed that line. There are highly effective twelve-step fellowships for almost all addictions nowadays, including Workaholics Anonymous, Alcoholics Anonymous, Narcotics Anonymous and Overeaters Anonymous. A quick online search will help you find one, or you could start by reading Russell Brand's book *Recovery*.[17]

---

17   R Brand, *Recovery: Freedom from our addictions* (Bluebird, 2017)

Energy Mastery self-test	3 Very rarely	2 Rarely	1 Often	0 Very often
I feel overwhelmed				
My to-do list is too long				
I am in back-to-back meetings				
I collapse exhausted in front of the TV at night				
I work evenings and/or weekends				
I drink more than two caffeinated drinks a day				
I drink alcohol more than two days a week				
I eat sugar and refined carbs to calm me down				
I'm in a rush				
I engage in compulsive behaviours to change how I feel				
I holiday less than I'd like				
I snap at people				
I exercise less than I'd like				
I drink less water than I'd like				
I drink alcohol to calm down				
I eat on the run				
I sleep poorly				
I feel stressed				
I have aches and pains				
I am moody				
I am physically exhausted				
I am emotionally drained				

Energy Mastery self-test	3 Very rarely	2 Rarely	1 Often	0 Very often
I feel lonely or isolated				
I feel restless and irritable				
I eat too much sugar				
Column totals: (Score 3 for very rarely, 2 for rarely, 1 for often)				
Add your column scores together to give you your **Energy Mastery score:**				

Your Energy Mastery score

If you scored 60–75: Congratulations, you have high levels of Energy Mastery. You are race-fit for the founder marathon!

If you scored 40–59: You are able to master your energy some of the time. Look at the Energy Mastery Toolbox at the back of the book for exercises to help you build more consistent and dependable energy.

If you scored 0–39: You need to strengthen your Energy Mastery. Prioritise the exercises in the Energy Mastery Toolbox at the back of the book.

Part Three Summary: The Two Elements Of Self-mastery And How To Hack Them

To survive and thrive as a founder of a scaling business, you need to show up as the best version of yourself. To do that, you need to be able to master your mind and master your energy.

Mind Mastery is about understanding how your subconscious brain works so that you don't get hijacked by your ego, fears and negative beliefs. In particular, you need to:

▶ Understand your ego needs and how to hack them (so they're not running you)

▶ Understand how negative beliefs work and how to dismantle them (so they're not running you)

Energy Mastery is about staying match-fit for the marathon not just the sprint. It's about taking care of your physical, emotional and psychological energy needs, in a way which is congruent for you. Three core ideas you can use to help you master your own energy are:

▶ The three energy tanks

▶ The stress-o-meter

▶ The first hour of the day

Questions to ask yourself

► What am I like on a bad day, and how is that impacting my team and my business?

► How might my ego needs, shadow behaviours and negative beliefs be getting in the way of my effectiveness as a founder?

► How well am I managing stress?

► If I knew my business success depended on me taking great care of my physical, emotional and psychological energy what would I do differently?

The Toolbox

In the Toolbox at the end of this book you will find a series of exercises which can help you manage your mind and your energy:

Mind Mastery Tools

1. Understand your ego needs
2. Identify your shadow behaviours
3. The do the opposite exercise
4. Dismantle unhelpful beliefs

Energy Mastery Tools

1. Fill the three energy tanks
2. Manage the stress-o-meter
3. Use your diary to manage your energy
4. Make friends with your parasympathetic nervous system

Next Steps

As a founder, you have achieved something amazing. You took an idea and from it you created something real. While some stood still and bemoaned the state of their life/job/world, you took action to change it. While others took the pay cheque, you took the chance. While everyone else saw the risks and the blocks, you ploughed through and gave birth to a new enterprise. You have a combination of vision, passion, commitment, bravery and determination that is awe-inspiring, and I salute you.

As you think about the future of the business you have given birth to, know one thing: what got you where you are, won't get you where you want to be. But you are tenacious beyond belief, and with willingness, a dab of humility and the tools in this book, the next stage of your venture can be as thrilling and successful as the start-up stage was.

The likelihood is that, while you may find most of the tools in this book helpful, you don't need them *all*. Most founders have one Achille's heel. For one person it's communicating to manage; for others it's Energy Mastery. One founder can struggle shifting between Brave Warrior and Considered Architect mode, while another finds that mastering their mood, ego needs and mindset is the greatest challenge. Having read this book you probably know what your Achille's heel is. Give as much energy and attention to that as you have to your product–market fit or investment, and I'd be happy to bet that you will multiply your, and your business's, chance of success by a factor of ten.

To survive and thrive as a founder you will need to challenge, and likely sacrifice, a couple of well-loved habits and beliefs, typically the belief that you are always right and the habit of being a lone wolf (two of the Brave Warrior's favourites).

Your chances of success will radically improve if you surround yourself with people who can support, mentor, advise and encourage you... and if you stay willing to listen to what they have to say.

I love founders, and my defining professional purpose for the past twenty years has been to help them not just to survive, but to thrive and succeed. If you'd like to find out more about my coaching programmes for founders, please visit www.thefounderssurvivalguide.com or, if you are a VC or a VC-backed founder, please visit www.vctalentlab.com.

"

Founders are unique
and brilliant, and
the founder journey
is a rollercoaster
of exhilarating
highs and crushing
stresses.

Go well on the
adventure with
my affection and
admiration.

THE FOUNDER'S SURVIVAL TOOLBOX

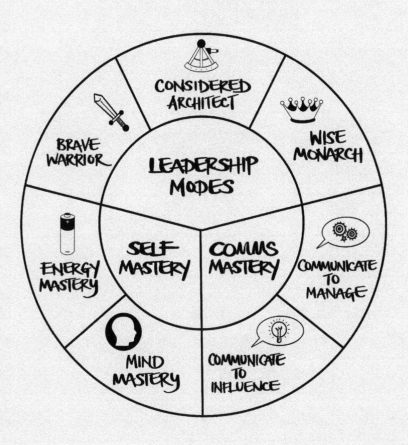

An Introduction To The Founder's Survival Toolbox

Having explored these three essential concepts of founder survival, the next step is into action.

If you're not sure where to start and haven't yet completed the self-tests in this book, begin there. Your scores will let you know where you need to focus first, and in the Toolbox that follows you will find a set of exercises to help you improve your score in each area.

If you already know that you need to build your Considered Architect mode, strengthen your Communicate to Manage skills or focus on Mind Mastery, skip to the relevant section of the Toolbox and start there.

You can also use the Toolbox as a resource whenever you face a challenge in your business. It contains many of the exercises I use most regularly when coaching clients and is designed for you to dip into whenever you need to.

The Toolbox Index

Brave Warrior Tools

1. Dial up vision
2. Dial up self-belief
3. Get the adrenaline pumping
4. Hang out with other Brave Warriors
5. Create a personal pledge

Considered Architect Tools

1. Introduce an annual cadence of business planning meetings (strategic planning and OKRs)
2. Delegate, don't abdicate
3. Think systemically
4. Think before you speak
5. Manage your focus

Wise Monarch Tools

1. Strengthen your strategic-thinking muscle
2. Think politically
3. Think culturally
4. Look up and out and build your personal board
5. Stay humble and in service of the business

Communicate to Manage Tools

1. Give good feedback using clean language
2. Coach for performance
3. Create a team charter
4. Introduce a team process review
5. Manage team dynamics

Communicate to Influence Tools

1. Think before you meet
2. Use the 5Ps to prepare for key communications
3. Structure your communication for maximum impact
4. Develop personal presence
5. Manage your investors or board

Mind Mastery Tools

1. Understand your ego needs
2. Identify your shadow behaviours
3. The do the opposite exercise
4. Dismantle unhelpful beliefs

Energy Mastery Tools

1. Fill the three energy tanks
2. Manage the stress-o-meter
3. Use your diary to manage your energy
4. Make friends with your parasympathetic nervous system

Brave Warrior Tools

Exercise 1: Dial up vision

The Brave Warrior is all about single-minded pursuit of a specific goal. Their drive to achieve that goal outweighs all doubts, fears, risks and potential blocks. Any activity that connects you with a vision of the future that excites and inspires you will increase your Brave Warrior energy.

Here are two ways to dial up your vision:

Future-pitch yourself

Imagine yourself in three years' time with the business of your dreams. Describe, in the first-person present tense, what your ideal day looks and feels like, starting from when you wake up. (Eg I wake up in my huge New York loft apartment feeling energised and ready for the day.) What do you see and do? Where do you work? What is your team doing? What do your offices look like? Who are your clients or customers? What are they saying about you in the media? Write as much as you possibly can, and get as creative as you can. Allow yourself to dream. Make it the most exciting, brilliant vision of the future you can possibly imagine.

Create a vision board

Use pictures and keywords that represent the business and life you want to build. You can include images of role models, meaningful words or phrases, financial targets, a picture of the office/shop/warehouse you'd like to have, a mock-up of your app as the highest download on the App Store, logos of the clients you'd like to win – the possibilities are endless. Again, make the vision board as inspiring and exciting as you possibly can.

Exercise 2: Dial up self-belief

The Brave Warrior has bulletproof belief in themselves and their business idea. If you find yourself feeling less than bulletproof, try these two exercises:

The 'I am someone who' exercise

Write 'I am someone who...' then complete the statement at least thirty times listing your positive attributes and strengths.

Do a self-belief inventory

Make a list of every single thing you have ever accomplished and/or feel proud about. These don't have to be Nobel-prize-winning achievements but aim for a list of between thirty and fifty accomplishments – from passing exams to learning to drive, from conquering a fear to taking your kids to Disney.

Exercise 3: Get the adrenaline pumping

If you are a fan of physical exercise, this is the time to give yourself that fist-pumping adrenaline high. The ultimate Brave Warrior sport is probably rugby, with squash a close second, but anything that gets you pumped-up will work. A challenging hill-climb on your Peloton, a brutal spin class, a treadmill sprint, even a hardcore Ashtanga yoga class can do the trick.

If you are not a fan of exercise, do a Haka instead. You might feel like an idiot, but it works. Look up the 'All Blacks Haka' on YouTube and copy that.[18] It is, after all, an ancient Māori warrior ritual to prepare for battle. It's the perfect Brave Warrior warm-up.

Exercise 4: Hang out with other Brave Warriors

You become the people you spend the most time around. If you want to dial up your Brave Warrior energy, identify five Brave Warriors in your network. Take them for lunch. Ask for their take on what you're dealing with. Get curious about how they think, act, hold themselves and speak. Authenticity is key here. Don't come straight back from lunch acting all gung-ho with your team if that's not you. Instead, just let their energy rub off on you a bit as you develop your Brave Warrior mode.

Exercise 5: Create a personal pledge

Most founders I work with are dab hands at crafting mission and vision statements for their businesses, but few have thought to do the same for themselves. In your business, a mission statement galvanises and inspires, and a personal pledge can do the same for you as an individual. It provides you with an anchor, an inspiration, a motivation and a reminder, and it fills the psychological and emotional energy tanks on a daily basis.

There is no right or wrong way to write your pledge because this is a private statement that needs to resonate only with you. But it should be challenging, inspiring and a reflection of your best aspirations. It should address:

---

18   World Rugby, 'The greatest Haka ever?' (2011), www.youtube.com/watch?v=yiKFYTFJ_kw, accessed 14 April 2022

- Your mission and vision for the business and for yourself as a founder
- The kind of founder, human, friend and family member you commit to being
- The standards, values and principles you will espouse

One useful brain hack I suggest you use is the 'first-person present tense, write as if it's already happened' hack. Your subconscious brain doesn't differentiate between real and imagined as well as you might think, so when you write as if you've already achieved your goals, it tricks the brain into thinking and acting as if success is guaranteed. A helpful way to do this is simply to start each statement of your personal pledge with the words 'I am'.

To write your personal pledge, take yourself off somewhere inspiring and unusual – a beauty spot, perhaps – and reflect on:

- The reason you get out of bed
- Your purpose as a human and founder
- What you want to achieve
- What you want to be known for
- The roles that you play
- The standards you aim to honour
- What's most important to you
- What makes you different both personally and professionally

Craft your personal pledge. Read it every day for a month. Here's mine as an example to inspire you on your journey:

Rachel Turner's Personal Pledge

- *I am warrior coach extraordinaire, 100% committed to the success of every person I coach.*
- *I am a passionate believer in the power of human connection to enable personal achievement.*
- *I am impacting the lives of hundreds of thousands of*

people through my work.

- ▸ *I am a brilliant financial provider for my family, team and future.*

- ▸ *I am a loving wife, mother, daughter and friend. I surround people with love and support.*

- ▸ *I am fabulous and fit. I take brilliant care of my physical, emotional and psychological needs.*

- ▸ *I am brave and kind, with a disciplined mind, a peaceful heart and a naughty laugh.*

- ▸ *I am a positive force in the lives of the people I meet.*

- ▸ *I am teachable, humble and of service to others. I remember that while I'm right, others are often righter!*

- ▸ *I work hard, am never boring and always colour-coordinate!*

- ▸ *I am only ever in control of my words, thoughts and deeds.*

- ▸ *I love life.*

Considered Architect Tools

Exercise 1: Introduce an annual cadence of business planning meetings (strategic planning and OKRs)

Introduce a standard cadence of annual, quarterly and monthly planning and performance review meetings and stick to them. Use this series of regular meetings as the vehicle to introduce change in a considered manner. Use it to engage your team with key decisions and plans, and to drive individual and collective accountability.

There are a multitude of different approaches to business planning, but the two I use most regularly with founders are:

1. **The traditional strategic planning approach:** Identify your strategic objectives for the next one, two or three years. Turn these into a six-month and/or twelve-month roadmap with key functional milestones, then cascade the plan to each department responsible for implementation.

2. **The objectives and key results (OKRs) approach:** The leadership team sets the organisational-level objectives and key results for the coming twelve months. Then each department or individual leader sets the ninety-day OKRs they will work towards in service of them.

The right approach for you depends on your business and the type of culture you want to create. If your business needs to plan more than ninety days in advance – if, for example, you have a seasonal business or long product launch cycles – the traditional model may be best for you. If you're in an emergent, fast-paced sector, for example, if you're developing software or a digital product, OKRs may be a better fit.

Whichever approach you choose, you need to introduce an annual cadence of strategy and planning sessions for you and your team. The typical business meeting cadence includes:

- An annual strategy off-site (two days) – to set and review your one- to three-year strategy and craft annual goals, milestones and a roadmap

- Quarterly review/planning sessions (half to one day) – to tweak direction, add new streams of activity, course-correct and set ninety-day OKRs or goals

- Monthly performance reviews (sixty to ninety minutes) – to track progress on ninety-day goals and activity on the roadmap

Exercise 2: Delegate, don't abdicate

Set your team members up for success by clarifying exactly what they are responsible for and what results they are driving in each quarter. Hold them accountable for delivering on these.

Role clarity requires more than a nebulous job description that sits in a drawer and is never referred to. When onboarding people, make sure they understand their job description, then agree their OKRs for their first ninety days. Check in with them monthly. Give them feedback, whether they're doing well or not so well. Regular, in the moment feedback is key alongside more formal performance reviews in the annual or quarterly calendar.

Exercise 3: Think systemically

In his seminal book *The E-Myth Revisited*, Michael Gerber asks founders to think of their business as a potential franchise, and to build a franchise manual.[19] A McDonald's chip tastes like a McDonald's chip anywhere in the world because every part of the process involved is written down in a franchise manual. The franchise model of business has fallen from favour in the past decade, but thinking of your business as a set of systems and processes which anyone could replicate is a powerful exercise.

Ask yourself the following questions:

▶ Which parts of the business could you systematise and how?

▶ What systems could you put in place to solve problems permanently?

▶ Which of your to-dos could you tick off by having a better system in the business?

Think about systems that will be appropriate for at least the next three years, not just for now – otherwise you will outgrow them as soon as they're implemented. For example, if you introduce a system to incentivise your sales staff, don't think of the system you need now, when you have two salespeople and a simple process. Think of the system you will need when you have twenty salespeople working on complex matrix sales projects with the help of numerous other people in the business.

---

19   ME Gerber, *The E-myth Revisited: Why most small businesses don't work and what to do about it* (HarperBusiness, 2001)

Exercise 4: Think before you speak

Not every battle needs fighting. You don't have to fix everything that bothers you, correct every mistake or right every perceived injustice. Before you act, remind yourself that when we're faced with something we don't like, we have three rational options:

1.   Accept the situation fully (without resentment).

2.   Walk away.

3.   Do something to change the situation (and we can only change what we say, think, feel or do).

Option four – seething with resentment while doing nothing to solve the problem and waiting for the other person to miraculously change – is not a rational option.

Often, the battles we want to engage in are ones we can let go of if we leave our pride, fear or ego out of the equation. But if you decide that you have to engage with a problem, because ignoring it would set a poor precedent or a bad direction for the organisation, or because you need to give someone feedback about their performance, then consider carefully how you want to engage. Ask yourself:

▶   What impact do I want to have? What is the change I want to create? What do I want to happen as the result of my engagement?

▶   Given the impact I want to have and the person I'm dealing with, what do I need to say/do and how do I need to say/do it, to achieve that?

Don't act rashly when you are angry, resentful, overwhelmed, stressed or afraid. Pause when agitated. Get calm. Decide what outcome you want to generate and what action you need to take to achieve that. *Then* act. Pay attention to the Mind Mastery Tools.

Exercise 5: Manage your focus

Coming up with new ideas during a marketing brainstorm, a product development session or a strategy off-site is brilliant. Diverting your entire team from their current work on a random Monday afternoon, just because you've just had a brainwave, may not be such a good idea, unless you're dealing with a crisis or rapid response situation.

Your team needs clarity about their direction, priorities and workflow, and you need to be the guiding light showing them the way. Don't be a sparkler – it may be pretty, but it doesn't illuminate much. Be a laser beam showing the path your team needs to follow.

Introduce new ideas in the meetings you have established as part of your annual cadence of planning sessions, and allow your team to reflect on how these will affect their current priorities and workstreams. Consider things like whether a new idea will require more resources, or whether you will need to slow down or pause other projects to make room for new priorities. Give yourselves a chance to think all that through before you divert the team.

Set up an 'ideas reserve' folder for any new ideas you have in between your standard planning meetings. Fill it with literal or digital Post-it notes, then review them and bring the best ideas to the team for discussion at your next session.

Wise Monarch Tools

Exercise 1: Strengthen your strategic-thinking muscle

Your strategy represents an informed choice about how your business will deploy its limited resources to the field of business to achieve your objectives. Your strategy lets your people know what the business will do and what it won't do. It provides everyone with a focus for their efforts.

When I'm coaching founders and teams, I can see the strategic thinkers in the room. While everyone else is talking about actions or system changes, the strategic thinkers zoom in on the one thing that will make the biggest difference.

To strengthen your strategic-thinking muscle, lift your view out of the immediate action plan to scan the whole game board. Look for trends, opportunities and threats, pose challenging business questions, future-pitch yourself and the business. There are a variety of models that you may find helpful. The faithful SWOT analysis, where you analyse your strengths, weaknesses, opportunities and threats, is a good place to start. You could also try a PESTLE analysis, to review the political, economic, social, technological, legal and environmental factors that may present opportunities or threats to your business, now or in the future.

Another way to think strategically is to ask the question: 'What business strengths do we have that we could double down on to create a competitive advantage and put clear blue water between us and the competition?' Get together with your leadership team and explore this question in a half-day blue-sky off-site.

Exercise 2: Think politically

Researchers Baddeley and James came up with an interesting political work matrix where they differentiated between politically aware and unaware people and those who are game-playing or acting with integrity.[20] When we think of office politics, we think of snide, manipulative, self-seeking and inauthentic people – these are the politically aware game-players, or what Baddeley and James refer to as foxes. You want to aim to be an owl, someone who is politically aware and acts with integrity. An owl understands that they need stakeholder support for their leadership, strategy and plan.

To grow your political-thinking muscle, ask yourself: 'How strong is my authority to act?' Produce a stakeholder map. Write down the names of all the people whose opinions and influence are important to your authority to act. Score each name red, amber or green on a scale from red, 'a saboteur who disagrees with my leadership, my perspective or my plan', through to green, 'an ambassador who is completely on side', with amber sitting somewhere in between. For each red or amber stakeholder, come up with an influencing plan. (See the Communicate to Influence Tools.)

Apply similar thinking to crucial or tricky meetings. Ahead of time, ask yourself: 'How strong is my coalition to act? Who in the meeting will agree with my proposals, who is neutral and who is outright opposed?' Think about how to build support for your ideas ahead of the meeting and/or how to tweak your messages to address the concerns and aspirations of the current naysayers.

---

20   S Baddeley and K James, 'Owl, fox, donkey or sheep: Political skills for managers', *Management Learning*, 18/1 (1997), 3–19, https://doi.org/10.1177/135050768701800101

Exercise 3: Think culturally

Culture is not something you can agree on in a strategic off-site then announce to the organisation and hope for the best. You and your leadership team are the DNA from which the culture of your organisation will grow. What you do and don't do, what you pay attention to and ignore, these are the things that establish the culture in your organisation.

Work with your leadership team to think about the culture and values you want in your organisation, then collectively explore these questions:

- ▸ How does an organisation that embodies these cultural values act?
- ▸ How do we as leaders model the culture we say we want?

You can't say you want a culture of innovation, then punish people who take risks. You can't say you want a high-performance culture if you don't hold people to account. You can't say you want a culture where people matter, then pay scant attention to onboarding, birthdays, festive celebrations and company events.

Exercise 4: Look up and out and build a personal board

Immerse yourself in stimulus and information from outside the operational engine of your business. Read trade publications, join professional bodies and build your network. It can be challenging to carve out time for this kind of non-urgent work when you're busy, but without an influx of new ideas, you'll get stale as a founder, miss opportunities and changes in the market, and innovation in the business will stagnate. Set yourself a ninety-day 'look up and out' goal, and carve out regular time in your calendar for it.

A personal board of directors can inspire you to look up and out. Think about building one, with members who fulfil each of the following roles:

- A peer – a co-striver whom you can turn to for fellowship and support

- A visionary – someone who will inspire you

- A super-connector – someone who will open doors for you

- An expert – a researcher, academic or policy-maker to bring intellectual challenge

- A diversity challenger – someone who will make you question your unconscious biases

- A mentor – someone who has succeeded in the role you are in and can share their experience

- An industry insider – someone who will keep you abreast of all the inside information

Be structured and proactive about your personal board. Schedule time to meet with each of them, ask for their support and offer your own support in return. Aim to meet with each member of your board at least twice a year. Be honest about what you want from them, and ask them how you can return the favour. Make sure the relationship is mutually beneficial.

Exercise 5: Stay humble and in service of the business

Spend time speaking to people at all levels of the business. Encourage honest feedback. If you're not already taking employee engagement surveys, start now and pay real attention to what you hear. Focus on what the feedback tells you about how *you* need to up your game, rather than on how others need to change. Remember that the only thing you can ever change is yourself – your words, your thoughts and your deeds. Welcome challenge and accept negative feedback as an opportunity to grow and learn. Stay humble.

Don't rock up in a Bentley, then plead poverty as you lay off 15% of your staff. Don't play favourites just because someone kisses your backside. Don't avoid essential meetings just because you find them boring. Think of yourself as a servant leader who draws on wells of discipline to give your people what they need to be successful. Leadership is not about what you want – it's about what your people need. Stay in service of the business and your people.

Communicate to Manage Tools

Exercises 1 and 2 are best for managing individuals, while Exercises 3, 4 and 5 are best for managing teams.

Exercise 1: Give good feedback using clean language

The next time you notice unhelpful behaviour from a colleague, peer or team member and decide that you have to address it, try this three-step process:

Step 1: Prepare feedback

Make sure you are in the right headspace. Get calm. Get outside the Karpman Drama Triangle (see Chapter 5) and check your negative beliefs and ego needs (Chapter 7).

Prepare your feedback. Be specific. Focus on actions, not personalities. Start by answering the following questions:

▶ What did the individual do? Be specific – eg 'He rolled his eyes in the meeting this morning', *not,* 'He's so bloody disrespectful all the time.'

▶ What was the impact of that behaviour or action – on you, the team, the meeting, the work?

▶ What would you like the individual to do more or less of in the future?

Step 2: Signpost feedback

It's important not to spring feedback on an unsuspecting person. Signpost to the individual that you'd like a feedback conversation with them. Send an email saying, 'Let's schedule some time to talk about today's meeting. I noticed a few things that concern me. I'd like to share some feedback and have a conversation about how we could improve things moving forward.'

Step 3: Deliver feedback

When you sit down with the individual, set a constructive, solutions-focused tone. Do this by repeating what you said in the email, verbatim.

Deliver your feedback using the following approach:

'When you... [their action], the impact was... [your experience] and my request moving forward is... [your desired solution].'

For example, 'When you rolled your eyes, I felt uncomfortable and I noticed the team shifting uncomfortably in their seats. My request moving forward is that you remain aware of the impact of your behaviour, speak up if you disagree with what I'm saying, or speak to me privately if you are frustrated or angry.'

When speaking about the impact of the person's behaviour, only talk about what *you* felt or observed. You can't speak to what other people experienced, and you don't want to find yourself in a debate about what the team thought of the person's behaviour.

Use clean language. Avoid words like 'should', 'always', 'never', and the accusatory 'you'. Start sentences with 'I'. Keep your tone neutral and calm. The statement 'I'm concerned about your attention in meetings and the impact that's having on the team' will get you a lot further than a charged-up 'You are *always* checking your phone and you *never* pay attention and it's annoying *everyone*' – even if the latter is just what you want to say!

Keep the conversation calm, constructive and solutions-focused. If the individual starts defending or debating, reflect that back to them and then re-deliver the three-step feedback above. 'I notice this conversation is getting heated and I just want to bring us back to my first comment: When you... the impact was... and my request is...'

If the individual is too upset or defensive, suggest that you pause the conversation and reconnect when they feel calmer.

Exercise 2: Coach for performance

Your responsibility when managing people is to elicit their best performance. You want people who can work independently, to as high a standard as possible, and that is much easier if you learn a simple method for coaching, not telling. When staff come to you with questions, the temptation to play rescuer and give your brilliant answer or advice will be great. Sometimes that's useful, for example, when they ask a specific technical question. But most of the time, you will elicit more high performance if you help them find their own answer.

You can use five simple coaching questions to help here:

1. What's on your mind?

2. What are you finding difficult?

3. What would you like to happen?

4. How could you achieve that?

5. How can I support you?

It takes practice to stop rescuing and start coaching your direct reports, but it will pay huge dividends in the long run.

Exercise 3: Create a team charter

Depending on the size of your team and how long you've been working together, this exercise could take anywhere from half a day to two days. If you have some challenging dynamics in the team, you will probably want to hire a seasoned facilitator or coach to run the session for you.

Your team charter contains your collective answers to the following questions:

▸ Why are we here?

▸ What is our goal?

▸ What are our 4Rs?

  ▸ What **roles** do we each have in achieving that?

  ▸ What **rules** do we honour in pursuit of that? (ie what are our operating principles/behavioural values?)

  ▸ What is our **roadmap** to get there? (ie what is our plan? What are our milestones? What are our goals/OKRs?)

  ▸ How do we meet to **review** this? (ie what is the ideal cadence and content of our team meetings?)

Please note the phrase 'collective answers'. Even if you think you know the answers to all the questions above, if you simply tell people what you think, their engagement and their commitment will be low. Start by asking others for their input, then guide and facilitate the conversation. If you feel strongly that something needs to be included or left out then say so, but if you begin by getting the team's ideas on the table, their buy-in will be much higher.

Exercise 4: Introduce a team process review

High-performing teams pay attention not just to what they're doing but how well they are doing it. If you want to prevent rumblings of discontent developing into full-blown dysfunction, the team process review is your preventative medicine.

Let your team know that in the next meeting, you'll spend some time doing a process review, reflecting on how the team is working. Send them one or two of the following questions to reflect on ahead of time:

- Do we hear from everyone in our meetings? How could we help others contribute more?

- Is everyone present and engaged in meetings? What would help people be more engaged?

- Is anyone's dominance impacting the effectiveness of our meetings and/or the accomplishment of our goals? How can we manage that?

- Are we able to express our views with courage and conviction in a way that's constructive? How could we do that better?

- How safe is it to express differences in this team? What would make it safer?

- How are we dealing with conflict? How could we deal with it more effectively?

- What one thing could we do differently to improve how this team functions?

During the meeting, facilitate, don't tell. Make a list of the ideas generated and make sure you act upon them.

Exercise 5: Manage team dynamics

Healthy, constructive conflict and disagreement is essential to a high-performance team. You need your team to be honest if they disagree with one another, and to be able to discuss any problems openly. Your role is to help the team have these conversations while staying in rapport with each other and critiquing ideas, not personalities.

A strong team charter and regular process reviews will help, but if you notice watercooler gossip, siloes in the group or disengagement in team meetings, you may need to intervene. As a first step, speak one-to-one with individuals using the feedback process above, but if you need to intervene in the middle of a team meeting, there are a few helpful things you can do:

▸ Suggest a timeout and remind the team of their operating principles. Use non-accusatory language, keep your tone neutral and ask the team to honour the operating principles you have agreed on. For example, 'I notice that emotions are running high in this meeting, and I want to remind everyone that in our operating principles we agreed to [x]'. Remind people to criticise ideas, not personalities, and to disagree with respect and courtesy.

▸ Do a thinking round. Pause the meeting and let the team know that you want to hear everyone's unvarnished point of view about a particular challenge or situation. Let them know you're going to pose a question, then ask everyone to share their thoughts, uninterrupted and without comment for up to five minutes each. Start with a broad and open question, eg 'What do you think or want to say about [x]?' Then ask who wants to go first. Let them know you'll hear from people clockwise from whoever speaks first, and that you'll set a timer to play chimes at the end of five minutes to encourage them to wrap up if they've not finished. Make sure you share your thoughts last.

▶ Call out unhelpful behaviour. 'I noticed you rolled your eyes, Mark. Tell me what's behind it.' Or, if you have two people who are loudly emanating at each other during a meeting, ask them to stay after and have a word with them. Eg, 'I'm not sure if you're aware of it but if there'd been thought bubbles over your heads they would have said "F off". Let's talk about what's going on between you, because I can't have that kind of hostility in team meetings.'

The other typical dysfunction you may need to deal with is when two team members come to you to complain about each other. They'll do this under the guise of wanting to keep you informed, but really they're looking for you to agree with their point of view or to referee so they can avoid dealing with the situation themselves. When approached like this by a friend, we typically listen and show we care. When you do this as a founder, however, you'll inadvertently encourage a culture of blame and dishonesty. Instead, use the five coaching questions above as a start:

1. What's on your mind?
2. What are you finding difficult?
3. What would you like to happen?
4. How could you achieve that?
5. How can I support you?

If they remain stuck, ask them outright, 'Why are you telling me this and what do you want me to do?' Challenge them to address this situation directly with the other person using the feedback approach above in the first instance. If they don't solve the problem, call a three-way meeting to explore the causes of and solutions to the dysfunction.

Communicate to Influence Tools

Exercise 1: Think before you meet

Think of a meeting, presentation or talk where you need to influence your audience. Ask yourself the following questions:

- What do I need from my audience?
    - What's the purpose of the presentation/meeting?
    - What do I want my audience to do/feel/have/say at the end of it?
- What does my audience need from me?
    - What do they care about right now?
    - What do they hope comes from the presentation/meeting?
- How is our rapport?
    - How do they feel about me/this idea?
    - How much engagement and buy-in do I already have?

Exercise 2: Use the 5Ps to prepare for key presentations or meetings

Think about a key meeting or presentation you have coming up. Use the 5Ps framework to think through what you will present or how you'll facilitate the meeting.

- ► **Step 1:** Get curious about your audience's **problem**. What's keeping them up at night? What's not working for them? What challenges are they facing and what's the impact of that on them/their people/their business? What is the problem they have that you/your idea may provide a solution to?

- ► **Step 2:** Think about what **pleasure** or aspiration they care about. What would success look like to them? What are the most important things they'd like to achieve or resolve? What would be the benefits for them of engaging with you/your idea?

- ► **Step 3:** Reflect on the **proof** that will matter to them. What can you tell them that will reassure them that your idea will meet their needs? What proof points are important to them, eg, do they need to see a roadmap, client testimonials, a product overview? Remember, it's the proof *they* care about, not the proof you care about. Leave your complex spreadsheets in the appendix.

- ► **Step 4:** Be clear what your **proceed to action** request will be. What do you want them to do as a result of the meeting? What's the next step? Make it as small and easy for them to act on as possible.

- ► **Step 5:** Once you're clear on the 4Ps above, think about what your **promise** will be. What deck title will grab their attention? What can you say in the first ten seconds to ensure they want to listen?

Exercise 3: Structure your communication for maximum impact

People form first impressions incredibly quickly.[21] Your audience is likely to decide within the first ten seconds of a presentation whether you are worth listening to or not, so the first things you say need to **GRAB** their attention:

▸ **Get their attention.** The very first words you say need to be surprising, exciting or important for your audience. (Having a great 5Ps promise will do this.)

▸ **Reason to listen.** Tell them the purpose of your presentation/talk, and what's in it for them.

▸ **Authority to speak.** If you are speaking to an audience who don't know you, establish your credibility.

▸ **Break down content.** Navigate the content you are about to share, using the power of three (see below).

For example, a low-impact talk might begin:

'Hi. Thank you so much for your time today. My name is Rachel Turner and I'm a founder coach. Today I'd like to share some of the things I've learned about founder survival.'

Transform this to a GRAB opening, and it sounds something like this:

'Up to 70% of start-ups will fail within the first five years. The purpose of this presentation is to help you make sure your business is one of the 30% that survive. My name is Rachel Turner and I've spent over twenty years helping founders survive, thrive and grow flourishing businesses. In the next forty minutes, I'm going to introduce you to the key elements of founder survival, namely leadership modes, communication styles and self-mastery.'

---

21   J Willis and A Todorov, 'First impressions: Making up your mind after a 100-ms exposure to a face', *Psychological Science*, 17/7 (2006), pp592–598

Once you've grabbed their attention, you need to keep it. Wandering off on a wild ramble through your thoughts won't do. Instead, you want to use the power of three to structure your presentation.

The brain works best with three bits of information at any time, and your subconscious will often chunk data into groups of three to help remember things – think about how you chunk your phone number into groups of three when you say it out loud, for example. Start by telling your audience the three key subjects you'll cover, then break each down further into three more chunks, and so on as needed.

Exercise 4: Develop personal presence

Albert Mehrabian's oft misquoted research showed that body language, facial expression and tone of voice were far more powerful in communication than we were aware. When dealing with communication relating to attitudes and emotions, he found that the degree to which we like and trust a communicator depends 38% on their tone and 55% on their body language, and only 7% on the words they use.[22]

To understand the role of body language in communicating gravitas and confidence, watch a video about a gorilla troop. You'll spot the alpha within minutes and it's not because of what is on their PowerPoint slide. Now, remember that we share as much as 98% of our DNA with gorillas and that we evolved for millions of years as walking apes ourselves before language burst onto the scene.[23] The human brain is genius at picking up the subtle nonverbal clues that tell us whether someone is confident or terrified, powerful or vulnerable, trustworthy or sly. And we think we're so clever with our long words!

---

22   A Mehrabian, *Silent Messages: Implicit communications of emotions and attitudes* (Wadsworth Publishing Company, 1971)
23   A Scally et al, 'Insights into hominid evolution from the gorilla genome sequence', *Nature*, 483, 169–175 (2012), https://doi.org/10.1038/nature10842

Much of our low- and high-status body language is actually the same as an ape's. A beta gorilla faced with a scary alpha and trying to avoid being attacked will adopt body language to make themself look less threatening. They'll make themselves small, avoid direct eye contact and slowly back away from the angry alpha. When we're scared of an audience, those old animal neural pathways in the brain fire up and we shuffle our feet (back away), hunch our shoulders (make ourselves small) and look at the floor or ceiling (avoid eye contact). Your brain is sending scared-gorilla messages to your body, and your audience experiences you as a low-status ape! Instead, you want to adopt high-status body language, just like the alpha in the gorilla troop. Stand tall, put your shoulders back, maintain direct eye contact and stay relaxed.

When it comes to tone of voice it's all about avoiding monotone and mono-pace in your presentations. You want to express emotion and vary pace, using pauses and speed to maximum effect. Great orators vary their tone and pace enormously to give their talks weight and impact. They slow down just before making a crucial point, and turn the volume up on a critical statement. In addition, tone and pace convey our intentions and our mindset. If my intention is to alarm or warn you of a danger, my tone will be sharp, my pitch high, my pace fast. If I'm trying to reassure you, my tone will be liquid and warm, my volume low and gentle, my pace slow.

One of the quickest ways to alter your tone and pace in a meeting is simply to clarify your intention. Try this. In front of a mirror, say the phrase, 'I love your presentation. You've done a great job.' Notice your tone of voice. Now say the same thing again, but this time dripping with sarcasm. Notice your tone. Then say it as if you've just found a winning lottery ticket in a ball of mush in the washing machine. Notice your tone. Finally, say it as if you're speaking to a beloved child. Notice your tone.

Now play around with different intentions. Try reading a shopping list with the intention to alarm your audience. Now try it with the intention to reassure. Lastly, try it with the intention to inspire and energise. Notice what happens to your tone, pace and body language.

Now try giving the first three minutes of a recent presentation in front of a mirror. Check your body language and facial expressions. Look out for low-status body language like hunched shoulders, jittery eye contact, lowered gaze, making yourself small, shuffling your feet or wringing your hands.

Next, try it again using high-status body language – plant your feet, hold your arms comfortably at waist height, make clear eye contact with your chin up and shoulders back. Aim to have a relaxed smile.

Record yourself in Zoom meetings or giving presentations. How do you look and sound? Are you calm and assured or frenetic and nervous? Do you command attention when you speak or simply fill the void with chatter? What does it feel like to listen to you? Energising and inspiring? Monotonous and dull?

Remember that people are watching all the time, not just in meetings and in presentations. What do you look like when you walk into the office or sit behind your desk? If you look frazzled, unkempt and stressed out, what are you communicating to your employees and stakeholders? If your desk and bag are overflowing with old food cartons and bits of paper, you will not exude gravitas and authority.

Pay attention to your wardrobe and your grooming. Every Wise Monarch understands the importance of costume and symbol. Whether they wear a Savile Row suit in Mayfair or socks and sandals in California, leaders communicate their values and presence in their choice of clothes. You want a wardrobe that communicates what you want to communicate and makes you feel a million dollars. If you know little and care less about clothes, hire a good stylist to help you craft a capsule work wardrobe or a Wise Monarch uniform.

Exercise 5: Manage your investors or board

This process owes more to the art of influence than the art of management as you don't have direct hire-and-fire authority over your board and investors. Key concepts to remember when influencing investors are:

▶ Remember they are not your buddies, your therapist or your peers. Their job is to protect the interests of the company in service of the stakeholders they represent. They look to you for leadership, strategy and results they can feel confident about.

▶ Don't hide bad news, but do share it thoughtfully. If investors discover bad news before you share it with them, it will erode their trust in you. If bad news comes as a bolt out of the blue you will struggle to hold their confidence.

▶ Triangulate and take counsel ahead of key board meetings.

▶ Manage board meetings. Send pre-reads and an agenda ahead of time. At the start of the meeting, reiterate the agenda. Bring the meeting back to the agenda if it drifts. At the end of the meeting reiterate the decisions and next steps. Send minutes.

Mind Mastery Tools

Exercise 1: Understand your ego needs

Step 1

Below you will find a list of ego needs. Scan the list and tick those that seem to resonate most for you. When an ego need is unmet, you are likely to feel uncomfortable, stressed, overwhelmed or fearful, so look out for words that spark those feelings for you. We often don't like to admit – even to ourselves – our most 'needy' needs, so watch out for the voice in your head that says, 'Oh no, I don't want to need that!' The likelihood is you've just found a deep-seated need.

Try not to analyse your choices at this point but simply go with your intuition. You can tick as many or few words in each box as you like. Tick every word which resonates as a potential need.

Step 2

Look at the three boxes where you have ticked the most words. These likely represent your three strongest psychological needs. For each box, pick one word that best reflects that group of words for you.

Ego Needs	
Approval	Freedom
Liked	Unrestricted
Regarded well	Independent
Recognition	Not obligated
Be praised	Self-reliant
Appreciated	Autonomy
Valued	Liberated
Cared for	Clarity
Understood	Assurance
Be helped	Certainty
Be treasured	Commitments
Be served	Control
Protected	Informed
Be taken care of	Order
Justice	Power
Do the right thing	Achieve
Not mistaken	Command
Loyalty	Performance
Honesty	Be busy
Frankness	Strength
Duty	Be right
Peace	Heard
No conflict	Be listened to
Balance	To communicate
Reconciliation	Be seen
Agreements	Be acknowledged
Unity	Be noticed
Calmness	To talk

Step 3

Understand where those needs come from. Most ego needs were developed in our formative years when we were powerless and dependent children. They often reflect the emotional scars we carry around in our psyche, which is why they can feel so raw when triggered. Look at your core needs. How are they a reflection of your formative experience? To what degree are they old scars and fears that still have sway over you today? Do you still really need these things – or does it just feel like you do?

Step 4

Spot when your ego needs are triggered. How do you know when a specific need has been triggered? How does it feel? What could you say to yourself next time they're triggered to remind yourself that these aren't true needs, they're just echoes of old scar tissue?

Exercise 2: Identify your shadow behaviours

Step 1

Think about yourself on a bad day. Tick any word that represents the shadow behaviours or thinking patterns you exhibit on a day like that. Feel free to add your own words.

Shadow Thoughts and Beahviours			
Aggressive	Evasive	Negative	Self-pitying
Aloof	Gossiping	Neglectful	Self-seeking
Apathetic	Grandiose	Obsessed	Short-tempered
Argumentative	Greedy	Opinionated	Shy
Arrogant	Guilty	Overcautious	Stingy
Avoiding	Hating	Overemotional	Stubborn
Belligerent	Headstrong	Passive	Submissive
Bitter	Hostile	People-pleasing	Superficial
Bossy	Humourless	Perfectionist	Thoughtless
Careless	Immature	Perverse	Timid
Cold-hearted	Impatient	Pessimistic	Uncritical
Complaining	Impulsive	Preoccupied	Unemotional
Critical	Inauthentic	Prideful	Unforgiving
Cruel	Inconsiderate	Procrastinating	Unfriendly
Deceitful	Inconsistent	Quarrelsome	Unrealistic
Defensive	Indecisive	Rebellious	Unreliable
Dependent	Inhibited	Reckless	Unscrupulous
Depressed	Insensitive	Resentful	Unthinking
Detached	Intolerant	Rude	Vague
Dishonest	Irritable	Sarcastic	Vain
Distrustful	Isolating	Self-centred	Vindictive
Dominating	Jealous	Self-critical	Vulgar
Dramatic	Judgemental	Self-important	Vulnerable
Egocentric	Lazy	Selfish	Withdrawn
Envious	Manipulative	Self-justifying	Workaholic

Step 2

Narrow your list down to ten words. Focus on addressing these in the 'do the opposite' exercise below.

Exercise 3: The 'do the opposite' exercise

Step 1

Take your top ten shadow behaviours and decide what the opposite of that shadow behaviour would be. For example:

Shadow	Opposite
Selfish	Service
Dishonest	Honest
Fearful	Courageous
Inconsiderate	Considerate
Arrogant	Humble
Greedy	Generous
Aggressive	Calm
Envious	Grateful
Lazy	Disciplined
Impatient	Patient
Resentful	Forgiving
Hateful	Loving
Harmful acts	Good deeds
Self-pitying	Responsible
Defensive	Open
Self-important	Curious
Withdrawn	Engaged
Suspicious	Trusting

Step 2

For two weeks, experiment with 'doing the opposite' every time you notice that your needs, fears and shadows have been triggered. Keep your list of shadows and opposites with you, and at the end of each day, note whether you were in shadow or opposite that day.

Exercise 4: Dismantle unhelpful beliefs

Step 1

Identify an unhelpful belief you are holding and how it's serving you. For example:

▸ Bob is an arse. This belief serves me because I get to feel superior to Bob.

▸ I'm no good at delegating. This belief serves me because I don't have to make an effort to try to get better at it.

▸ The investors will never go for that. This belief serves me because I don't have to risk the investors saying no.

Step 2

Recognise that this is just a belief, just like 'the sun goes around the earth' was once. It is not a scientifically verifiable fact.

Step 3

Make a list of ten pieces of evidence that contradict the belief. For example:

▸ Bob is good at accounts. He's pretty good fun. His team like him. He supported me in the discussion with [x]. He's got a good heart, etc.

▸ I could learn to delegate if I tried. The work on Project [x] was well delegated. I'm good at clear communication, which I know is important for delegating, etc.

▸ The investors have surprised me before. I could make a good commercial case for this idea. If I engaged with and built more rapport, they may be more open to my ideas. They invested in [x] radical idea before.

Step 4

Ask yourself: 'What would I do if I believed the opposite?'

Step 5

Do that!

Energy Mastery Tools

Exercise 1: Fill the three energy tanks

Step 1 – Imagine you have three energy tanks representing your physical, mental and emotional energy. On a scale of 1–10, how full is each tank?

Step 2 – For each tank, identify the activities or habits you engage in that are most depleting.

Step 3 – For each tank, identify the activities or habits that would most fill the tanks.

Step 4 – For the next week, remove one depleting activity/habit and add one nourishing activity/habit.

Exercise 2: Manage your stress-o-meter

For one full workday, track your stress-o-meter revs. Each time you go to the bathroom, put the kettle on or get a glass of water, pause. Ask yourself: 'On a scale of 1–10, how stressed and adrenalised do I feel?'

Notice what a 7 or 8 feels like. Maybe you have a dull ache in your solar plexus. Perhaps you feel like you've had five espressos. Maybe you start getting short and impatient with everyone, or your mind is racing and can't settle to anything.

Identify the things that increase the revs. For example:

- Lots of caffeine
- Rushed diary

- Saying yes when you should have said no
- Not enough time between meetings
- Brooding on something that has happened or might happen
- Negative self-talk
- Running late all the time
- Trying to do too much too fast
- Poor prioritisation
- Lack of support
- Lack of systems
- Watching the news
- Skipping meals
- Being overtired
- Arguing with people

Think about what you could do to reduce your revs. For example, you could:

- Cut out coffee
- Reduce sugar
- Drink no alcohol on a weeknight
- Leave ten minutes between meetings
- Limit the number of meetings you say yes to in a day
- Take time for a proper lunch break
- Practise a simple breathing technique
- Take a ten-minute nap
- Listen to a guided visualisation
- Meditate for ten minutes
- Take a walk
- Book a massage at lunchtime
- Do some stretches

- Sign up for a lunchtime yoga class
- Book an after-work training session

Keep your revs below a 5 for a whole day. Make that your number-one priority for the day. You may notice that, if you do that first, everything else becomes first class.

Exercise 3: Use your diary to manage your energy

There are myriad approaches to time-management, task-management and diary-management out there, and I won't repeat them all here. Suffice to say that you will radically improve your focus if you spend time reviewing your tasks, plans and diary:

- Annually – reviewing your progress and strategy, setting annual goals
- Quarterly and/or monthly – tracking progress and setting your focus for the coming quarter/month
- Weekly – identifying and diarising your important, not just urgent, tasks
- Daily – clarifying the three most important tasks for the day, and tackling the worst one first

These moments of diary, plan and task review also provide you with an opportunity to reflect and tweak your self-care and energy habits. As you review your progress in the previous quarter/month/week, ask yourself what conditions have allowed you to be at your best, then use your diary as a way to schedule those things so they become routine. You may choose to block off time in your diary to:

- Take a ten-minute break between meetings
- Have no more than five hours of meetings a day
- Block the first hour at your desk to do deep-thinking work
- Schedule regular lunch breaks

- ▸ Book personal training sessions or classes to bookend your days
- ▸ Schedule a weekly no-meeting afternoon
- ▸ Schedule a monthly 'inspiration lunch' with peers or colleagues
- ▸ Book a quarterly minibreak to refresh yourself

Exercise 4: Make friends with your parasympathetic nervous system

Stress is the founder's constant companion and the fight-or-flight response it triggers is one of the biggest threats to your ability to survive and thrive as a founder. When stressed, your heart rate rises and your body floods with adrenaline and cortisol, all of which interfere with your decision-making abilities. When stressed, you make mistakes, miss clues and become more impulsive, less productive and less effective at managing relationships.

The parasympathetic nervous system can turn down the fight-or-flight response, so your ability to turn that system on will be central to your ability to manage yourself, your leadership and your communications. There are many ways you can do this, few of which will appeal to you if you're a stressed Brave Warrior founder! They all involve slowing down, which can feel counterintuitive when you feel like you have to speed up. But whether we like it or not, the old adages of 'More haste less speed', 'Measure twice, cut once', or 'Slow down to speed up' are absolutely true. (Thanks, Mum.)

To turn on the parasympathetic system, you need to find a way to calm your mind, slow down your thoughts and access a sense of peace and calm. There's no one right tool for everyone. Experiment with some of the ideas below and find one that you can practise daily. The more you practise, even if it's just for five minutes a day, the easier it will be to access your parasympathetic system during moments of stress.

Use simple breathing techniques

▸ Box breathing: Imagine a box and trace the outlines of the box as you breathe in for the count of four, hold for the count of four, out for the count of four, hold for the count of four.

▸ Counting breath: Breathe in for the count of one, out for the count of two, in for the count of three, out for the count of four, and so on, until you reach ten. Keep your counting and breathing slow and regulated as you do this.

Practise meditation or mindfulness

▸ Use an app like Headspace or Calm.

▸ Watch a YouTube video – a ten-minute guided meditation or visualisation exercise is a good place to start.

▸ Buy some mala beads (or worry beads or prayer beads – I don't think beads care what denomination they are) and use them while reciting a short mantra. Your mantra can be anything you like, but some examples are: 'In with calm, out with stress,' or, 'Help me be kind and brave.'

▸ If you belong to a religious denomination, you may find that repeating a traditional prayer can help you calm your thinking and relax your mind. I'm a non-practising, non-monotheistic Roman Catholic and find the 'Prayer of St Francis' very soothing.

Moving Meditation

Any activity that stops your thoughts bouncing around your head like a bumblebee in a Perspex box are good. You may find that swimming or running are your route to calm the mind. My personal favourite is yoga, with Hatha, Yin and restorative yoga being particular favourites.

If you know you lack the discipline to practise meditation or mindfulness on a regular basis, set up some external accountability. Hire a yoga teacher, join an online meditation group, buddy up with someone and chant on Zoom once a day – whatever floats your boat. Just make sure you do it!

Acknowledgements

If we are like the people we spend the most time around, I got seriously lucky to have Roger and Jan Turner as my parents. Dad, you taught me to be a Brave Warrior. Mum, you taught me that I could do anything I set my mind to. The unconditional love, unwavering encouragement and unquestioning support you have given me has been the bedrock upon which any success I have had in life has rested. I love you both deeply and forever.

To my husband, Francesco Furriello, you have been the centre of my universe and the place my soul calls home from the moment I met you, midnight, New Year's Eve 1988, Love at the Wag. You are my other half. *Ti amo da morire.*

William Furriello, it has been the greatest honour in my life to be your mum. You are an extraordinary human being, and you fill my heart with happiness every single day. Your passion and compassion, insight and warmth, creativity and determination are awe-inspiring. I adore you. And thank you for saving my life.

To the Lychetts posse: to Alex, for being the second son I never had (love you, mate) and to Rachel, Gareth and Helen for putting up with us motley crew, thank you.

To the people who made this book possible: Siobhan Costello for your incredible patience and coaching. Joe Gregory, Anke Ueberberg and Kathleen Steeden at Rethink Press for sticking with me when the edit got tough. To Rachel Cone-Goreham for your wise counsel. To Polly MacKenzie, without whose feedback this book would be a bit shit. To Rob Kaplan, Petronella West, Rachael King, Dilek Dayinlarli and Melanie Travis for reading early drafts of this book and giving me honest feedback – and gorgeous praise quotes.

And an extra special thank you to the hugely talented Tom Russell at Inky Thinking for the fantastic illustrations in this book.

To my partner at VCTalentLab.com, the incomparable Kevin Greenleaves. Thanks for putting up with my Brave Warrior mode and for modelling Wise Monarch. And to Alan and the team at The Table Group, thanks for the team wisdom you bring to our Brave Warrior clients.

I have been blessed to be surrounded by some real professional wonder-women in the past two decades:

Elizabeth Dunne and Victoria Jeyaratnam, you are the power behind the throne. Elizabeth, thank you for picking me up when I was on the floor, and always making me look good. Victoria, thank you for keeping me propped up and for taking better care of me than I do of myself. I cannot overstate how much of my success is due to the support the two of you have unfalteringly provided over the past decade. Thank you from the bottom of my heart.

Ginny Baillie, you are my best buddy, and it's been a privilege to walk the coaching road with you every day since 1999. Love you.

To my coaching compatriots Ann Wright, Una Murphy, Paula Seabourne-Pearson, Carole Gaskell, Fiona Houslip and Nadja Taranczewski, thank you for your inspiration, partnership and wisdom through the years.

Thank you to Sophie Dummer, Suzanne Robinson, Susie Russell-Smith, Anja Birnbaum and Roberta Rampazzo for your friendship and care.

And an honourable mention to some pretty amazing men too: Brian Bates, Ben Turner, Carl Cox, Paul White, David Walker, Lee Gorton and Mark Nelson-Smith. You inspire me.

To the crew who keep me sane: Bill, Bob, David, David, Patrick, Bryony, Heather, Danielle, Tim, Harry, Amy, Faith, Alex, Carmel, Sean, Becca, Michelle, Ali, Kevin, Suki, Kefi and many, many others. I am so grateful to have you in my life.

Last but not least, thank you to the founders and leaders I have worked with over the past twenty years. It is a rare privilege to have been invited into your lives and your businesses. I am humbled and grateful to have worked with so many amazing people, and to have had an opportunity to make even a small impact in your lives.

The Author

Rachel Turner is a founder and 'Alpha Whisperer' with more than twenty years' experience as a transformative coach and leadership, team and culture consultant.

She started her professional life as a music industry entrepreneur, founding five successful dance music enterprises with her then partner DJ Carl Cox before her twenty-fifth birthday.

Having achieved great start-up success and been instrumental in the careers of some of the world's top DJs, she struggled to lead her businesses as they grew and ended up leaving the music industry in the mid-nineties. She completed a degree in applied psychology, trained for two years as an executive coach and has spent the past twenty years helping clients avoid the mistakes she made as a founder.

Rachel established her coaching practice in 1999 and has since coached thousands of people to break their own internal glass ceilings. Her superpower is coaching entrepreneurs who need to scale themselves to scale their businesses.

In 2020, she co-founded www.vctalentlab.com to put leadership talent development at the centre of the VC ecosystem. VC Talent Lab helps founders of VC-backed companies optimise their performance and includes global investment funds and fast-growth tech companies among their key clients.

Rachel serves as a senior advisor on behaviour change to global/multimillion-dollar organisations. She is passionate about impacting leaders who impact the world and tithes a percentage of her professional time to not-for-profit organisations.

Rachel is married to her teenage sweetheart Francesco and splits her time between their homes in the Sussex countryside and Soho, London.

🌐 www.vctalentlab.com

🌐 www.FoundersSurvivalGuide.com

in www.linkedin.com/in/achieveunlimited

◎ @thefounderssurvivalguide